# Poetry without Tears

First published in 1959, *Poetry without Tears* is a book not about what poetry is. The author argues that this book is not concerned with the educational resurrection of a dead art but about the artistic resurrection of education. Poetry is a force released in activity. That is how an educationalist and a poet see it. It is rarely how critics and academics see it. They see it as a series of poems, correspondingly it is as a 'Collection of Poems' that it is taught. Basic educational truths are frequently overlooked in our teaching of the arts, and no art suffers more from this than poetry. Baldwin goes on to say that in the end teaching is a creative activity and the creators are the best teachers. This book is a must read for students of both literature and education.

# Poetry without Tears

Michael Baldwin

First published in 1959
by Routledge & Kegan Paul Ltd.

This edition first published in 2024 by Routledge
4 Park Square, Milton Park, Abingdon, Oxon, OX14 4RN

and by Routledge
605 Third Avenue, New York, NY 10017

*Routledge is an imprint of the Taylor & Francis Group, an informa business*

© by Michael Baldwin, 1959



**Publisher's Note**
The publisher has gone to great lengths to ensure the quality of this reprint but points out that some imperfections in the original copies may be apparent.

**Disclaimer**
The publisher has made every effort to trace copyright holders and welcomes correspondence from those they have been unable to contact.

A Library of Congress record exists under LCCN:

ISBN: 978-1-032-64071-6 (hbk)
ISBN: 978-1-032-64073-0 (ebk)
ISBN: 978-1-032-64072-3 (pbk)

Book DOI 10.4324/9781032640730

# POETRY WITHOUT TEARS

by

MICHAEL BALDWIN

ROUTLEDGE & KEGAN PAUL
London

*First published 1959
by Routledge & Kegan Paul Ltd.,
Broadway House, Carter Lane, E.C.4
Printed in Great Britain
by Latimer, Trend & Co Ltd, Plymouth*

# CONTENTS

# ACKNOWLEDGEMENTS

A TEACHER is perpetually in debt to his colleagues and pupils; it would be impossible to estimate or record how much. The substance of this book has been in some way derived from every one I have ever taught. I cannot say whether it has received its shape from those of my colleagues with whom I agree or from those who have honestly and consistently urged their judicious disapproval. I would not willingly forfeit my association with either.

More estimable debts are owing to: J. McGill Clouston, Esq., O.B.E., B.Sc., Headmaster of St. Clement Danes Grammar School, London; Major E. R. J. Barlow, M.B.E., T.D., of Colyer Road Secondary Modern School, Northfleet; H. W. Sayer, Esq., of St. Paul's College, Cheltenham; and to John Holmes, whose knowledge of strip cartoons is even greater than my pupils.

From among the latter I must specially thank all of those whose work appears in the following pages.

H. W. Sayer, a fine artist and a great teacher of art, once said to me that young people's work should not be exhibited. Poetry, however, sets itself different problems of communication and has less tangible blemishes and perfections. I have tried only to print work that will stand positive and unashamed in its own right and in a mature context. There is no 'bad' work included, though I have tried to explain how bad work can be made good work. People do not compose poetry in order to have their failures publicized; most of us are happy if what we consider our good work is acclaimed.

'From when I was at the age of about eight, I started to read poetry and I have never left off. (*AT SCHOOL MOSTLY. SOME AT HOME*)

'Once I made a little book, and wrote poems in it.

'I didn't write much poetry at my old school, but we read a lot. They were mainly balads.

'I prefer to write poetry than to read it. (*THAT GOES FOR ALL ENGLISH.*)'

'On a whole we did not read much poetry together but we had a period when we copied out poems that we liked from a poetry book.

'I prefer writing poems to reading them.'

'I think I would rather write poems than read them. I feel, when writing poems, that I can suit the mood I am in myself; and in that way like poetry and not think of it as dreary. At the moment I am twelve years of age.'

# In General

# 1. SUBJECT

I F POETRY can survive fifty years of mass education it can survive anything. It has been misrepresented, maligned, misnamed, misunderstood and deliberately mislaid; its anaemic double discovered on calendars and coo'd over by maiden ladies with cups of tea. Patience Strong and Matriculation Boards have done their worst; but it is still published. If it sells badly, then it always sold badly—to start with; and quite recently we've started with several poets who are now selling well. If bogus verse had its big successes in the last century (just as some of the poetry of that age which now sells well had its incredible failures), so it has had amazing sales in the last ten years. 'The White Cliffs' is just as good a bogus poem as 'Enoch Arden', and 'The White Cliffs' sold two million copies.

I am not going to discuss what poetry is; for poetry, whatever it is, is thriving. This century, as last century, some pretentious verse (and it is none the worse for that) is selling rather well, and next century the real poetry of this century will be selling even better. The critics can quarrel, but the poets and the educators have got to get on with it.

I have put it like that because this book is not concerned with the educational resurrection of a dead art. If it were discreet to flaunt paradox so early I would like to say that it is really about the artistic resurrection of education.

Poetry is a force released in activity. That is how an educationalist and a poet see it. It is rarely how critics and academics see it. They see it as a series of poems; correspondingly it is as a 'Collection of Poems' that it is taught. But surely, it is something emerging from the individual; not something existing outside and demanding to be let in.

Basic educational truths are frequently overlooked in our teaching of the Arts, and no art suffers more from this than poetry. Education consists of enlarging areas of recognition: the mind is encouraged to progress from the boundaries of its own experience. Yet the most usual method of teaching poetry is not to call upon what the child has within, but to present it with a 'poem', which one hopes, generally in vain, to be close to its own experience.

The sciences are intellectual; the arts emotional and instinctive. Therefore one would expect the teaching of the sciences to be intractable and forbidding and the teaching of the arts fluid and stimulating. Unfortunately for the Arts and to the great credit of the sciences the reverse is true. Initially, in teaching the sciences, universal systems are demonstrated to manifest themselves in common experience. The rules that govern gravity can be introduced in such a way, for example. In our teaching of the Arts, on the other hand, we confront the child with those most intractable objects, adult works of art. There is nothing, or very little, in a child's mind, or to a lesser extent in an uncultivated mind of any age, to relate it to a statue, a poem, or a piece of music. But all children have within themselves in differing degrees the desire to create plastic forms, to express experience in words, and to make music or, to be cynical, the noises out of which music is made.

In contemporary teaching of Art and Music these instincts are gratified far more successfully than in the teaching of literature. Art schools are crowded; a fair proportion of people develop at least their interpretive skills in music by learning an instrument; but go to a university and inquire how many people read poetry, even among those studying English Literature, and the number is very small. Inquire among those who teach English at schools and the proportion is still disappointingly small.

It can be objected that it is unfair to equate Art and Music with Poetry rather than Literature in general. But General Literature in every time-table I have ever seen has included masses of poetry. Even if more penetrating arguments cannot be found to support my case, the mere fact that poetry is so frequently taught by people who do not like it should be sufficient. The more educated members of the community, the educators, have manifestly been inadequately educated, and yet the system insists they pass on this inadequacy. Far better stop teaching poetry altogether than teach the painful painfully.

But my real argument rests in the nature of the fallacy I noticed a moment ago: the fact that poetry is disliked in school, but literature at large is still quite widely enjoyed. Why is this, and what does it mean?

The inference I would draw is that general literature, novels, biographies and so on, is more resilient to the inorganic system of teaching now practised. The reason is twofold: the first is that adventure is less fragile than poetic experience; the second, and greater, that the pupils know more literature than their teacher can spoil for them. An insistence on the merits of those adult totems, Dickens or Thackeray, may cause a temporary retreat to Leslie Charteris or *The Eagle Comic*, as indeed the insistence on the merits of Leslie Charteris and *The Eagle Comic* would quite certainly compel a further withdrawal, but the terrain is wide and provides ample room for manœuvre. When people leave school they return to the wide fields of literature. Poetry, on the other hand, is a word which represents armed frontiers. From it the pupil retreats rapidly, and towards it re-advances cautiously. He never re-enters it, because all he has seen of it at school is a vast and forbidding desert. Unlike literature at large it can be made barren in the classroom by a single word.

If this were all the damage, I should be content to let poetry in the schoolroom die. I should certainly put aside my memories of class reactions to poems that have been enjoyed, a reaction far more positive than to anything else in literature; and I should also stop writing poetry. I should even forget the more metaphysical concept advanced later, dear to a theorist but to no one else. But I said earlier that poetry is a vital creative force; and it can only be inhibited in school at the cost of great damage to the individual and to the cultural balance of society. What is that damage?

Literature without poetry is the neatest mathematical expression of it; but this does not mean merely literature at large without the poetic in form. It means a lack of awareness of the poetic in substance; an experiencing of great literature without the means of its greatness. It means that literature will be enjoyed not for what it is but for what it represents, and it would be free to represent it in an increasingly shallow manner. It would be like judging a painting solely by the criteria normally applied to a photograph.

Is this, in the widest educational terms, important? Undoubtedly it is. If the Arts are to have any educational value it must be in their ability to enrich the approaches to knowledge and experience, and to make the art of experiencing its own sort of knowledge. Other subjects enlarge knowledge and experience directly; if the Arts are to relinquish their greater indirect function they will have no value at all, and in any event they will lose the richness that makes them possible classroom material. I believe that these simple considerations reach deeply into the heart of our cultural life; but there are others equally profound.

We live in the age when words are cheap and constantly being cheapened further: the slick slogan, the bare headline, the advertising catch-phrase are all forces at work to atrophy imagination. Only a fool would complain about such things or pretend that they ought not to exist. They certainly ought not to exist by themselves, however. Science itself is important in educating us to reach the truth of words, but very often in a scientific age we do not know enough to judge the underlying propositions upon which truth is supposed to rest. It is literature, and more especially what is poetic in literature, that educates us in the quality of words, and it is from this factor and this only that we can equate sincerity of language. Our only concepts of Faith and Belief in the widest sense are artistic rather than logical ones.

People frequently object to poetry because it is 'different'. Yet it is its essential 'difference' that makes it an educational expedient, however much educational method seeks to disguise it.

In the poem there exist in concentrated form habits of thought and expression which other media dilute and dissipate. No novel, no play, no film, is without its poetry; though it is rarely desirable to point this out to a class, since such comments are not very likely to stimulate interest or perception. Yet once the individual is possessed of a poem, he has 'the thing itself'. Everything else he reads is enriched by this single fact. An education in the virtues of prose is a bore. From the child's point of view it is like being asked to study the contours of a steppe. An education in the 'virtues' of a poem is no doubt equally boring, and this book does not suggest such a prosaic method. The poem is its own education. Geography teaches itself in the hills.

Such remarks will seem terribly trite to those who believe in poetry, and will not, I suspect, go far to convince those who do not. For the latter I have this to say. During a pupil's least articulate years he achieves poetry far more readily and at a far higher standard than he achieves prose, and such composition liberates prose. Why and how such results are obtain-

able I will explain in a later chapter. For the moment here are
two poems by a boy of eleven:

THE BAT

A moth flits,
A bat swoops,
Soundlessly.
A lamp gleams
And moths,
Attracted,
Fascinated
Helplessly dash themselves
Against its sides,
To fall,
Lifeless,
To the ground below.

The bat circles,
And suddenly twists:
Two buff-tip wings
Flutter to the ground.
Again he turns
And wings his way
Silently
To rest on a branch—
Forked, skeleton-like branch,
Of a lightning marred
Desolated tree.
Whose bleak boughs
Look like the horns of the devil
Against the moon,
A golden coin in the sky.

BRIAN M. SHARPE

*Subject*

### THE SKELETON'S STORY

'I was a seaman once'
The skeleton said to me,
'So loyal to my vessel
While she was out at sea.

And while the storms were brewing
And we were down below,
The ship around was slewing
No fear did I show.

In the hills and valleys of the seas,
I stood, iron shod,
While my mates were on their knees
Praying for help to God.

When the ship was cleft in two
And men leapt in the sea,
I was the last man of the crew
From the stricken boat to flee.

All men went down unto their graves
But one clung to a spar,
And kept his head above the waves,
'Twas I! I floated far.

The terrible storm was not abating
The seas they slashed around,
The spar along the waves was skating
And yet—I was not drowned.

But then—in answer to my prayer,
A sail, it did appear,

## In General

To snatch me from those watery lairs
For death itself was near.

But when we came to port, I said
"I'll go to sea again,
I'll fight the waters till I'm dead,
I'll battle with the main!"

I sailed the seas for eight years more
Then wed a captain's daughter,
I settled down and studied law—
Forgot about the water.

But soon the sea grew strong in me
'Twas like a burning pain,
The challenge—thrown out by the sea
Sent me to sea again.

This time I joined a whaling boat
To hunt beasts so prolific,
We were attacked by pirates
While in the South Pacific.

I fought them like a demon
Wielding a great sword,
Till a pirate flung a club
That knocked me overboard.

I hurtled down towards the sea
Knowing I had no chance
I cried, "Thou sea—you'll not kill me!"
And plunged down on my lance.'

The skeleton told me all of this
He told me all his story

*Subject*

He now glows with a great white light
And rises up to glory.
                    BRIAN M. SHARPE

And here is a piece of prose obtained by the 'poetic method'. It was elicited by a colleague of mine, Mr. Michael Purser, and therefore proves that the methods I advocate are neither restricted nor personal.

### IMAGES OF THE GALE

A door banged shut as if by a hidden force, like a giant gong of doom; as if it knew the peril and danger that lay outside. It was trying to stop us getting into the house. It was as if someone had shot an elephant.

The wind blowing against my window that night was like a madman trying to wrench it open. I could hear Indian war drums beating. A hundred ghosts were slamming the doors of doom. It was like echoes from the dead.

While I was asleep, the wind went on blowing as if it wanted me to have nightmares all night long. I dreamt there was a war on. It was out to destroy everything, as if a man wanted to hurt me and I was waiting for him to do so.

Next morning, the wind was still blowing, as if I had woken up from a bad dream to find it had come true. It was like turning the radio on full. It was like a recurring number. The trees outside my window looked like goats butting at me. The branches seemed to be tormented by some great invisible hand. The trees looked like drunken men, they were jellies wobbling. The trees were like flames leaping from a furnace, or a lady's hair being blown by a drier.

My friend and I went out for a walk, and the air smelt like ice, like a battlefield after the battle, like wet salt, seaweed being pulled up, a builder's yard. The wind pulled at my clothes as if it wanted them and they didn't belong to me. It was like a giant magnet pulling at a piece of steel, or the moon attracting the sea, or a vacuum cleaner. It was an octopus clutching a frogman, an eagle attacking its prey, cats fighting for some fish. I felt as if I had been caught in a rose bush, as if a lunatic was trying to rip them off. A snake seemed to coil round me.

My friend tried to speak to me and he sounded like someone shouting in the distance, someone standing at the end of a long passage and calling to me. His voice sounded like a gramophone record going very fast or very slow; it sounded like someone trying to talk under water; like ghosts whispering in my ear; an elephant trying to speak; a feather dropped on a pillow. We began to whistle but the wind was stealing the notes away; a hand pulled the tune out of our mouths. It sounded as if arrows were whizzing past us, like the wind itself. It was the lost chord.

We saw a house with one of its chimneys blown down. It looked like a camel without a hump, a business man without his bowler, a bottle without a neck, an elephant without a trunk, a man without a head, a birthday cake with a candle missing. It was like a wrecked ship, a dejected monster.

Other people walking along with their heads down looked as if they were going to a funeral or were searching for some money they had dropped. It was a dream in which everyone had been beheaded; they were leaning towers under the sea. They were spacemen worked by remote control, headless puppets, tortoises with their heads in, people with aching necks, bulls charging, ants scattering, boys in disgrace.

We saw some washing on a line and it was like ghosts writhing in torment, or captives trying to release their chains, or clouds tied to a pole. The clouds in the sky looked like big white bulks of death. The birds moved like snails; they were trodden-on shuttle-cocks. The overflowing gutters were tubes of glue being squirted all over the place. The water in the river was a poisoned leg swelling and swelling. My raincoat felt like slime over a dead man.

After the gale, branches and twigs lay on the ground like dead snakes or dead fireworks. The clearing sky looked like a piece of paper being torn slowly down the middle. The clouds were like spectators being moved on by the police after an accident. They were like ice cream being thrown in all directions; curtains being drawn back; an army in retreat; a box slowly opening. At last the sky was a blue swan.

CONTRIBUTED BY FORM II

There can be little doubt about a system which produces such material; and with such evidence I am content, for the present, to rest my case.

Except to say this. What has been gained has been gained from the pupil. Nothing has been put into the pupil, for he does not need it.

A person who has given this is already very well equipped to deal with major literary problems. He writes more convincingly than far older pupils who have been taught by formal methods. He is obviously in a good position to judge the words of others.

If a person can express one thing he can express another. Images are easy but thoughts are difficult; but with the vigorous expression of what is easy, what he has inside, comes confidence, and he quickly learns to express things in general.

The language of feeling is an easy language for the child to learn. The language of feeling is poetry.

He likes what he makes himself, so he likes poetry.

Poetry as religion, philosophy, unacknowledged political forces, poetry as a 'criticism of life', poetry as a paper game of words: all of these ideas are important because people have believed in them and acted on their beliefs.

There is another way of regarding poetry. It does not matter if it is not a very logical way; its truth can be approximately demonstrated and it has no corollaries to call for closer definition. All that is necessary is that we should act on it as seriously and vigorously as these other untruths have been acted upon. I refer to the idea of poetry as an education.

Education is not a very pleasant word, even to educationalists; and I see no reason why it should appear any more pleasant to poets, even though great poets have been concerned for centuries with teaching us to use our feelings, and even though most of them were concerned with making our minds more 'aware' rather than more 'organized', and thus themselves qualifying as educationalists rather than philosophers or moralists.

Of course, any art form that has to be kept alive at school ought to be allowed to die: but poetry is not being kept alive at school; it is being killed. Not by neglect but by eager misrepresentation.

Yet the true educationalist ought to be able to do well for poetry.

His aim is to enlarge the awareness of others, and because of his more objective concern he is far more sensitive to failure than the artist or critic. That is why, given the opportunity, he is the best possible advocate for poetry, or for the Arts in general. He is not concerned with subjecting them to any processes other than those his pupils evolve for themselves, to meet the needs of the poem or painting in question.

That does not mean to say that he is not interested in morals or criticism or philosophy. Of course he is. He is certainly not interested in compelling his pupils to accept any particular system, any more than any particular poem or painting, or *compelling* them to accept anything else.

If he is a propagandist at all, and he is only in so far as he controls the order in which things are set forth, it is that he would prefer people to like rather than dislike, and to feel something rather than nothing.

His aims are remarkably similar in this respect to the creative artist; but this, let me hasten to add, is not all of my reason for writing a book about education and poetry. I am not an advocate of 'the related theme'.

No: poetry matters to education and education matters to poetry. Such a conviction is not the haphazard result of being both a poet and a schoolmaster, for it may well be that I am not very good at either of these pursuits; but of a number of arguments that I prepared to state at length.

All of the Arts play an important part in practical teaching. Each of them adds its own dimension; and of them all literature has perhaps the largest contact with everyday values, so it is certainly an educational necessity. I have already shown that poetry is a very effective way of meeting this necessity, and if I can show later that it is an enjoyable and easy activity in the classroom, then it will also follow that it is an unavoidable expedient.

It can be objected that the usual school-anthology poem is unlikely to enlarge the appreciation of any values other than its own, and that these are rather hard to detect. I agree. The school anthology is generally unmitigated boredom. I am talking about poetry with a point of view.

The 'poet of repute' with his assured sale of perhaps a thousand copies may wonder at all this. He is honest enough to confess, I hope not brag, that his is an esoteric art; but quite certainly most of the poets of my acquaintance would deny that poetry should owe its life to the schoolroom. Such an art deserves to die. What they do not realize is that good poems are being killed stone dead daily. Let them come with me and I will show them the most horrible outrages being done to the Muse by mealy-mouthed murderers and back-handed assassins.

For, after all, my educationalist *was* a legend. I hope he has so far been taken no more seriously than any other image of what we seek to be. We fall from grace; but like the Tinker rebuked by the Rector we can at least ask who she is.

Poetry suffers from bad teaching more than any other art. This is not because it is less resilient, but because it is more open to abuse. 'English' is a subject central to any curriculum. 'Poetry', alas, finds itself in the amorphous area indicated by that all-embracing word on the time-table. Fancy being taught poetry by the man who teaches you grammar and précis. Fancy being *taught* poetry; which is instinctive with all of us —'before puberty' say the cynics. 'Before senior school' cries the poet, and I believe he is right.

One more thing: I do not expect to be able to persuade either the schoolmaster or the poet very easily of the truth of what I shall say. Both of them, both of me, have survived the systems I seek to attack. Why should they worry? It is for the other thirty-five people who were once in their class that I write, and for their successors. The man who likes a subject is the last person to consider educationally. Ask Smith minor why poetry is a bore and he will tell you. After you have had time to dissuade him from this most natural belief ask him *how poetry should be taught* and he will say the only words on the subject that are worth hearing.

In the end teaching is a creative activity and the creators are the best teachers. We need to pour our creators into our schools, our training-colleges and our departments of education. They will do more for Education and for the Arts than they will at University or in the Academies.

We have encouraged false ideas of progress and cultural growth based upon formal virtues. In the end progress depends upon what happens in the mind of the boy who leaves school at fifteen to pick up a spanner. If you commercialize culture the masses are right. Today the convinced minority is an anachronism.

A formal education in the Sciences may mean everything. A formal education in the Arts means nothing; it is doubtful if it ever did. We must go on teaching Science and stop teaching the Science of the Arts.

What we must replace it with is what this book is about.

# 2. TEACHER

No training college, university, or university department of education offers an adequate training for teachers of English. Most authorities are agreed about this; and I am not trying to belittle their excellent work by stating a truism so directly. The subject itself is so large, its aims so diverse, that perfect training is almost impossible. When good teachers are encountered they seem to be accidentally endowed; one realizes that they could have been given nothing by training, nor, alas, would they have anything to give to another teacher if they were appointed lecturers. They have enthusiasms, backgrounds, histrionic abilities, far beyond the ordinary run; and these things cannot be received or given. It has been our own good fortune to be taught by them, or by someone like them. That is why we are interested in English ourselves. Only a very few can hope to be like them, and only a very few can hope to be successful teachers. What can the rest of us do, those of us who cannot perform prodigies of mimicry in front of our classes, or imbue the dead word with living fire? What can be done for us and what could our training have done for us?

It is because of this inadequacy that I am writing this book. I do not write it with so impertinent an object as to 'educate' the lecturers; because, in general, they agree with what I say. It is their misfortune to be part of a pattern of events over which they have no control; and for themselves to break the pattern would achieve nothing, since they only see their pupils for one or two years, at the department or the training college, and by then a formal system of education has already done its worst. At best they can only suggest and modify, in the hope that a pupil will try their suggestions at least once in the classroom and be won over by a reaction which he is generally too inexperienced to notice. A trainee teacher who has won his academic distinctions with difficulty is never very responsive when he is told that he must now learn not to teach what he has learned. Education is conservative because its educators have had to suffer it. In such a context, experiment always seems fraudulent, and it is rarely recommended by the obviously light-weight mental equipment of some of the experimenters. A young teacher arrives at his first appointment to be asked what training college or university department he attended. His answer is always greeted with: 'Well, you can forget *that* nonsense. At *this* school . . .'

Yet to teach poetry is really a very simple business. In the old days a pupil would walk with his mentor or seek out a prophet in the wilderness; he would see, or hope to see, a practical demonstration of living in grace or at least in truth. The rainbow or the worm in the stone would be a shared experience. He would learn a little from living.

Nowadays we turn collectively to Exercise One. We understand the prism of the rain and the making of fossils. We are rich in the jargon of analysis; but deficient in wonder, which is the first step to synthesis. Neither analysis nor synthesis, art nor science, are exclusive; neither seeks to limit the other; neither can be dispensed with. . . .

We know all of these words, because they are a paraphrase of all the words on modern education, modern sociology, modern psychology, modern anything, that we have ever read. They are very true words but they ring no bells in the brain. They represent the problem so we can certainly be excused for forgetting it. I am more concerned with the answer.

Nearly everybody who reads poetry has tried to write poetry at some time or other; many people read because they are themselves private practitioners; many others have found that the identity that the reading has given them has often sought to express itself in writing. Many of these people have stopped writing because inner conviction or external persuasion has suggested that they are not quite as good as they hope to be; but that is not really the point. The point is that considering the smallness of its audience poetry numbers a remarkably high proportion of prospective practitioners among it.

This is not purely relative. Obviously, of course, a novel does not provoke such a high percentage of its total readers to imitation, but it could be argued that a novel with an audience of ten or twenty thousand is going to embrace a far wider public than a poem with its comparatively limited audience, that the novel in fact reaches people who would not feel themselves called upon to emulate anything. The novel, it can be said, reaches many of those who are purely receptive; the poem only reaches the creative.

Actually, for every sort of reason, this is not true. It will be found that there is something in the very nature of poetry that challenges imitation: the smug sonnet is often as provoking as an anagram or a crossword; people—all sorts of people —react to the challenge of *verse* itself. They often founder because *verse* is all they have been educated in, or because of sarcastic discouragement from teachers, friends, or their own reading circle. But they do try.

I am not really concerned about these people for the moment, however; I merely cite them as the sort of evidence most of my readers recognize. Most of my readers will at some time or other have tried to write a poem, I am confident of that; but since they are the sort of people who will trouble to read a book on poetry, they are also, quite obviously, not the people my book is about. If through them I can reach those that the book is really concerned with, however, I shall be rather more satisfied. And they are reachable.

For I shall now make my second assertion. Many more people write, or try to write, poetry than actually read it with any consistency. A lot of those most ordinary, even semi-literate, people occasionally write verse. For verse is, after all, the medium of the semi-literate. It is a pre-literate medium. For example, much of the Heroic and Ballad poetry now extant was composed by people who could not write. This is a rather vital pointer to practical teaching, and it obviously has ramifications far wider than the mere teaching of poetry. I shall return to it later. For the moment let me record a few simple facts.

When I was an Army Educational Instructor, although I was interested in poetry, I did not start off by intruding it into the classroom. My reasoning was that my main problem was to teach men and enlisted boys to read and write and do simple arithmetic. Many of my own instructors had told me, and I agreed and still agree, that when one is dealing with under-educated people even the lowest aim is noble. What I did not realize at the time was that poetry is not the highbrow thing that I then thought it to be and that most education-alists and certainly most of the educated insist that it is. What I did not know was that most people want to come in contact with poetry, whatever the word means to them, and they only recoil later when the contact or the manner in which it is made does not fulfil their expectations.

It was soon apparent in the case of these men who were starting their education anew or even for the first time that they regarded literature and poetry as nearly synonymous terms. So some poetry they had to have. I was prevented from making any mistakes of the sort that the later part of this book warns against, merely by force of circumstance: I could only give them a limited amount of poetry because time and my conscience would not let me give more. So the fact that I chose unwisely and dealt even worse did not result in too much harm.

These men and enlisted boys were rather a special problem. Education had not really penetrated their defences either for good or for bad, as far as I could see; so I do not want to linger upon their request for poetry any more, other than to point out that infants and juniors at school who are educationally in a similar position, though psychologically and intellectually so different, also start by responding warmly to poetry. Could it really be that environment, age, intellect, have very little to do with the whole matter of poetry; and that our system of education itself is the only bogey? I believe it could. But I anticipate.

My teaching was actually done with a specialist unit, where it was likely that the general intelligence would be above average. Most of the men in the ranks, many of these of too good an educational background to be my direct concern in the context of Army Education, were against 'poetry'. I knew their interests, their reading matter (if any) and so on: they were against 'poetry'. It was a word with a very bad meaning for them. They had been taught before.

Only a word. In one particular barrack-room there was a Kipling and a Robert Service on a shelf, and most of the men in that barrack-room read Kipling and Service. Kipling and Service were not poets; they were men. In spite of differences of background the subjects were recognizable and masculine. This wasn't 'poetry', but something else. I very quickly became obsessed with the idea of doing away with the word 'poetry' in education if I wanted to get anywhere with poetry itself.

But these tastes were accidental and not shared by other men in the camp. That Kipling and Service had needed to be physically introduced. Most men in the forces, most people anywhere, will idly pick up a book and flick the pages over. But the book has to be there. In the case of every other hut it was not there. Again, these men were in their middle thirties and living communally, a condition of age and society that induces reflection, but which is, all too obviously, not general.

The real revelation came later. Two men, quite independently, brought me poems they had written and said they wanted my opinion. One claimed he wanted to enter a competition in the *Soldier*, but was still rather embarrassed; the other one had no reason at all for bringing it to anyone except that he had written it and I was probably for his mind what the medical officer was for his body and the padre for his soul. We all take our poems and our problems to someone. A poem for most people is a very considerable problem. He too was rather embarrassed, but here he was.

Fortunately, and it was fortunately, for I was a bumptious youth with my own first book of poems soon to come out and no educational precepts to guide me whatsoever, fortunately I took my cue from the embarrassment and said that the poems were very good, that the man concerned must write more, and so on. If either of them had come up challengingly, as does a person who has just produced something he cares about but wishes to pretend otherwise, I might well have said as a schoolmaster had said to me on a similar occasion, 'Arrange your participles correctly and then you will realize how inferior you are to Gray'.

I was encouraging and they wrote some more; one or two people in their hut wrote also. They didn't like 'Poetry' but they wrote poetry.

All of this was a very eloquent testimony to the fact that most of our teaching of the Arts leaves very many powerful energies unharnessed. It was educational testimony; and its application to the classroom will follow in due course. What is lacking is some cultural testimony, for it is upon this that education in the art depends—the idea that one is encouraging a communion with living values rather than a scrutiny of dead ones.

In this case the cultural testimony came in unlikely guise at the smoking concert. I will pass over the playlets, the sketches, the musical items, and the funny man—though surely even here there are wider implications—and come to the 'poetic' part of the programme. 'Received' art was represented, because a very plump sergeant did a Stanley Holloway recitation; but 'creative' work was even more in evidence. The sergeants sang a ballad, apparently specially composed or re-composed each year by the Regimental Sergeant Major, on the accidents of day-to-day existence in the unit; a corporal recited some verses on comical characters at the camp; and a sallow-looking soldier who was obviously highly regarded leapt up and proclaimed that he would recite two dozen unseemly limericks, at least six of which he would guarantee as entirely fresh because he had just written them himself.

Art begins and ends in entertainment; one can refine upon one's pleasures infinitely, but however much one persuades oneself that the celebrated Cantos in the Paradiso represent a far higher sort of pleasure than the tap-room limerick, one should realize that unless the same psychology is at work in the appreciation of both of them neither pleasure could exist. Verse, in the widest sense, is not dead, in spite of fifty years of mass education. If it can survive that it can survive anything.

It will be objected that verse and poetry are not the same things, and this really provides me with my main point. We brutally shock men away from 'poetry', presumably by a too liberal application of *Daffodils*, but they embrace 'verse', of the good salt variety, completely of their own accord. Obviously there are creative boundaries, but surely there are other points of contact?

To speak in parables: there was also a sergeant-major of signals who read only pornography. He was the best read man I have ever met. His approach to the world's greatest literature was perhaps a trifle oblique but his quest had led him to it all.

This would seem to lead us to a point no further than to say that our teaching should take more from the pupils and be a lot more sympathetic to their likes.

In abstract this is very ordinary fare indeed. In practice, however, every teacher of English I have ever met ignores these obvious educational principles when dealing with poetry.

In plain terms he

Doesn't know how to get pupils to create poetry.

Doesn't believe it would do any good if he did.

Doesn't know what his class would like because he has not yet found anything that his class does like.

Would not know where to find poetry the class would like even if he knew what it does like because, as I mentioned in the last chapter, he has either acquired his own taste for poetry the hard way or just as likely acquired no taste for poetry at all.

This last fact is undoubtedly true and on the face of it would appear to make the whole problem unanswerable.

If comparatively few English teachers do read poetry out of school, what right have they to insist on the merits of poetry to a class? It has not, in their eyes, merit enough to be part of their own lives. How can they begin to judge what will give pleasure to others? Where will they discover the energy to communicate pleasure, where will they derive the impetus to look for suitable material, and how will they be able to tell when they have found it?

For the moment these must be left as rhetorical questions. There is an answer, and it is not to suggest that they start reading poetry, or even (far more reasonably) that they stop teaching it. For the moment I am interested in the other class of teacher: the teacher whose liking of poetry is indiscriminate; that is the teacher who does not understand poetry, either in real life or the classroom. In other words, all of us.

Our attitude probably originated at school. It is varied in its origins, but almost certainly one of two things happened to help promote it. The most likely is that English (and whatever we understand by this word can probably be traced back to school also), however our particular school or schoolmaster defined it, became something we could 'do'. We obtained good marks; it became, in a comparative subject system, *our* subject. The teacher noticed us kindly. We took to the teacher (as schoolchildren we always responded warmly to the person who flattered us) and his word became law. Poetry was part of his word, so it became law. English was our subject: Poetry was our subject. We enjoyed the crossword of transferred epithet and Miltonic inversion, we smirked at the boredom of the class, and they put up with us tolerantly. After all, we were bored in Physics, weren't we? And someone has to answer the questions put to us by our daily array of fools. Better to share out the chores. For the saved and the fallen alike, culture existed uneasily on a par with Boyle's Law and equilateral triangles. Now we are schoolmasters.

What we assimilated without protest, since it has led us to a fuller and more abundant love of poetry in our maturity, we are prepared to give without question. If boys do not like 'Drake's Drum', there is nothing else for them to like, not from poetry as we understand it. One boy will like it, just as we did. After all, in the new town, we should count ourselves lucky if our class produces one such person. As young men we turn our energies to producing more than one; as we grow older we turn merely to him, our furtive familiar. We have survived a system that showed us the truth. Surely that truth must be perpetuated?

*But what is the use of poetry in the twentieth century?* Can we answer that? It cannot be snuffed out, this desire for creation; poets still crop yearly in the politer bookshops; but most of them are as distant from Tennyson as Tennyson is from the wishes of the class. Until we can see anything permanent about it, until our teaching leads towards permanence, how can we teach?

Surely the only form of culture that can be propagated is that which entertains a certain number of people. In the classroom all that can be propagated is that which entertains the majority of the class. But poetry as we know it does not entertain. As adults we read it, those of us who do read it, because it prompts reflections quite unrelated to mere entertainment. In other words, as we know it and love it, poetry is not for the classroom; yet our total educational aim must be to make it appear a pleasant habit.

Later on I will show that, given the correct attitude, this is not so hard to achieve. But what of us? We need to change in ourselves. I would like to suggest that those teachers who are failing with poetry try to learn just a little from their classes.

This is not to advocate inertia on the part of the teacher and demonstrative anarchy on the part of the class, as some imperfect practitioners would seem to imply. If one is to progress at all in the teaching of the Arts one must be not merely an observer: one must have an observable viewpoint. An essential factor if one aims at doing little oneself yet encouraging much in others is that the relationship should be reciprocal. One does not stand over a class but the class should know where one stands, and, indeed, what one stands for.

In the next chapter I shall discuss 'aims' in a purely tactical sense: the sort of approach one makes to the class and how one should regard that approach. The key to this will be found to be the simple one that poetry is to be enjoyed, that activity in the English lesson in general is to be enjoyed. But such an attitude must start with the teacher.

There are two main motives for teaching, and they both have their own dignity. One can like one's subject or one's pupils. Ideally one does both, but this ideal state always reveals itself to be a sort of bigamous triangle with oneself the unhappy focus of conflicting loyalties, and it is all too easy to become either pedant or pedagogue and discard one's less-congenial affection.

It is only when one sees that the needs of the subject and the needs of the class are the same that one is in a position to resolve this conflict. In other words, when one comes to see the subject as a force which can be found in the class and which does not need to be transmitted to it one is in a position to begin.

If poetry is alive then it creates itself and once it does this it creates the answer to the problem of teaching it. When a boy wrote for me,

> An express train at night is like a jewelled snake,
> Writhing round the curves in the track.
>
> A goods train is like a line of dirty men,
> Plodding home after a hard day's work.

he enjoyed doing it, and the class enjoyed hearing it because they had been busy with similar things themselves. I enjoyed it even more than any of them because I have read a lot of poetry but never anything like that, even though every day boys write lines as good as that.

I had all the energy there, all the introduction for any

English lesson formal or informal I could possibly think of. If I had started by giving the class a poem I should have had nothing. But now they will come confidently to any poem I offer and accept it or reject it, as a craftsman looks at the work of another and judges it inferior or superior, without ever once calling the craft itself to question.

The theory is as simple as that, and in practice it will never fail. Indeed a person who agrees with me absolutely and knows how *he* would go about the whole thing with his class need read no further.

The strange thing is that the application of this idea does not stop at school, though it is at school that the changes must take place. Even at university one is educated to a 'one down' attitude in the presence of a poem: every seminar or poetry-class I ever attended oozed a peculiar atmosphere of caution, largely because one was invited to look 'more closely' at works one had already seen. At Harvard, I am told, Professor X takes a poem and locks a pupil in a room with it. This may be the *reductio ad absurdum* of everything I am attacking; but its moral is clear. Our present system of education leads us step by step to a point where we can do anything with a poem except read it and enjoy it. 'We must not *write* poems because we do not *know* how to write poems. Shall some one teach us?' The sequence is so wrong that obviously the answer is 'no'. And I warn anybody anxious to prove *me* wrong that if he charges into his classroom and asks his pupils whether they want to write poetry their resulting raspberry will not demonstrate my error in the least. It is not quite so simple as that, even if he *had* started aright when he first met his class two years ago.

However, let us suppose that this overall creative approach is the wrong one, and consider the alternative for a moment. I am going to talk about English teaching in general, because the teaching of poetry is a part of one's

English teaching in general. All must be taught well or nothing survives.

As one prepares oneself to be an English teacher, or as one prepares a group of lessons, one is faced with a most obvious question: what can one give?

The glib answer is: a great deal. At grammar school level, for example, there is enough formal grammar to keep a class busy for three years; then there is punctuation, figures of speech, précis, paraphrase, several different types of composition, several hundred progressive and graded admonitions; not to mention all one's work in literature ('work', mark you), plus one's personal acceptance or rejection of the poetry problem, which somehow, whether one is for or against poetry as a person, always seems curiously isolated from everything else. If it does not appear as a rather special problem one is probably insensitive; and if one treats it as a separate problem one will certainly be a failure. In any event, one is to be excused for supposing, as one takes stock, that there is a great deal of complete and complicated material to be communicated.

This purely formal attitude will not do, of course. We all know this instinctively, and this book is certainly not going to labour what has been obvious in theory and practice for a long time. There are very few English teachers today who are happy to conduct a formal course, and I am not going to pretend that there are, just to provide myself with an easy target. But unfortunately very few of us are completely at ease with a less formal approach either. We feel like swimmers who have left the barren for the vegetated shore, but who are also conscious that with the barren shore we have left dry land far behind.

And that more inviting bank is a long way away. Some of us flounder in the middle and some turn back; and of the two groups the latter is generally better off, for they come back determined to make the best of a bad situation. At least they know where they are, and how to go about things. There is considerable experience behind them and a renewed conviction. Most of us, however, continue to flounder in the middle.

In simple terms: we have abandoned formal lessons on the topics I have indicated above, and we have done so confident that our pupil's reading and composition should provide the centre of our work. The reading gives motivation to composition, and we only teach formally to answer problems that crop up in the latter. Everything is tidy and logical, and we are now teaching empirically.

This sounds very well, and in theory it is far better than the old formal method. Yet to anyone who has any real knowledge of handling the subject in the classroom, it is arrant nonsense.

Its unworkability depends upon the unnatural emphasis it places on composition. In order to obtain enough talking material, or enough material to occupy the class so that one does not have to talk too much, one either has to insist that masses of written work are done or spend a lot of one's time commenting on the written work that is done. Both of these alternatives are very boring to the class; and the second, seemingly easier, option from the pupils' point of view has the disadvantage that they soon come to regard endeavour as a mere prelude to exposition. Follow this method, and one simply cannot fill in the time without loss of momentum, or without resorting to Fabian tactics with one's literature, such as indulging in reading round the class (a gross waste of time, as well as an unforgivable abuse of one's pupils' possible enjoyment of the book in question); or even re-inflating the subject by teaching it formally.

How, then, does one reach that other shore?

Both the formal and the more enlightened method have this in common: they both seek to reduce errors of taste and composition. The former does it by teaching rules; the latter by correcting examples. They both set out to eliminate what is bad, rather than to cultivate what is good.

This is the point at which the good theoretical education-alist will want to interrupt me with considerable violence. Surely, I am arguing towards a truism? My answer to this is twofold. It is a very profitable direction in which to argue if it is indeed a truism, and especially if it is a neglected truism.

And in the case of English it *is* neglected. Whatever its general application, one wonders whether, in this particular instance, it is a truism at all. Unless error is eliminated, the education is not complete. English is not a subject in which strength can be developed to compensate for weakness. In an adult style, genuine grammatical weaknesses mean, quite simply, that there is no strength; they also mean that an education has failed.

Besides, English comes in academic trappings, even in scientific trappings. Clause analysis, say, is a scientific opera-tion. And in the sciences, no matter how much one teaches through encouragement, one quite simply cannot afford to proceed to a fresh proposition until the preceding one has been assimilated. Correct punctuation is far harder to teach than Boyle's Law. The problem is on a gigantic scale. Hence the excuse for carefully eliminating the error before proceed-ing. It is argued that one simply must have a firm basis on which to build.

The fallacies in this are obvious enough; but the resolving of them is a different matter. Hence the floundering. Hence the distance of that farther shore.

Yet the remedy is so simple, and its adoption means that the difficulties are set immediately aside. Composition is an artistic endeavour, or the right sort of composition is; and it is a principle of artistic endeavour, and of artistic education, that errors are not eliminated but outgrown. The first and most obvious treatment of a stylistic solecism is to ignore it, and to encourage something not of it but applied to it. One does not ignore it because one does not wish to tackle it formally, or because one is frightened of showing up the class; nor quite certainly because it is irrelevant. One ignores it because a good style can be encouraged to grow far more easily than a bad style can be eliminated by negative methods.

For the moment, what I should like to say is this. The change must come in the classroom, not the lecture-room. Only when people grow up to a new conception of English education will change have any meaning. And the classroom must engender this change because it is something within the child we are seeking to liberate. In Chapter 4 I shall prove conclusively that this 'something' is there.

The starting point is obviously with the very young, for these have the greatest enthusiasms. Yet contrary to many people's convictions these enthusiasms do not disappear by themselves as children grow older, though they are subject to modification. What generally happens is that they are blasted by the insensitive comments of teacher and parent. A child does not need to be treated like an elaborate hot-house plant, and I am not going to suggest that we need to invest in bag-fulls of bogus psychology. Encouragement is cheap enough, and is easily practised by the sensitive and insensitive alike. Anybody having anything to do with children need only encourage and forget his doubts about whether or not he is an expert in the subject under discussion. Encouragement is the one unharmful attitude. It is a frightening thing to realize that, to young children at least, all adults are experts.

But we have not time to worry ourselves into being experts. The creative work of younger people in literature should be the schoolmaster's main strength. The teacher whose critical ideas on poetry are vague will not have to proceed on trust very far with the methods I advance before he is completely won over on educational if not on cultural grounds.

Of Picasso it is frequently objected that a child could do as well. This may be nonsense. Somewhere in that remark, however, lurks the idea that the child with his freshness, his vigour, sets down a very similar challenge. Two generations of mature painters have not admired the work of children for nothing. They know that the child has artistic perceptions that are stifled in the adult. Such perceptions may be the result of the child's raw approach to his medium; that is, they may be accidental. But education should take advantage of these blundering discoveries of power. The teacher is concerned primarily with what exists in the pupil.

I spoke earlier of 'understanding poetry'. That is a very portentous phrase, as well as a nearly impossible condition; and it was intended more as a warning than as a sign. We can never know enough, never know what is the right knowledge, so we are all equally inexpert, and should all equally look for new material to enrich our teaching—but the plain truth is that our teaching is most likely to be enriched by itself. We must beware of preconceived notions, and be careful of the 'expert'. The man who 'knows his subject' is almost as big a danger to education as the complete ignoramus: and at present we are producing both sorts of teacher in like proportions.

'Poetry lovers' are generally horrible highbrows, save when they are merely wet. The sweet old lady with her autographed Felicia Hemans is not very likely to harm anyone at school, but the dedicated old men with their iambic walk, and the young men with their pockets full of Fry can do a great deal of damage.

Culture is in the power of that most uncultivated person, the schoolmaster. He must create, not admonish. He must move with the times. His main need is not to know but to help to know. A good teacher of the Arts need, in one sense, know nothing at all. If he teaches them as knowledge or as existing in knowledge he enters the realms of error. Nine English teachers in ten, whether possessing university qualifications or not, are quite certainly not qualified to teach poetry formally. They don't know what it is. None of us knows. All we can do is abandon our error and attempt the informal. It is easy to find inspiration in the child.

*In Particular*

# 3. AIMS

THERE IS only one aim in teaching poetry in the class-room: that is that the pupils should enjoy it. If there are any more speculative aims, of the sort we discussed earlier, they exist outside the classroom and can only be served through enjoyment.

Unfortunately poetry is frequently prostituted to serve the following functions:

*To train memory.* Some schools have a weekly 'Memory Homework' for junior forms. Such a policy is so muddle-headed that it is not surprising to find that it generally takes the convenient form of learning a piece of poetry by heart. The English teacher, who is supposed to be responsible for his class's enjoyment of literature, has to listen to thirty or forty recitations, waste a whole period in frustration, boredom and frequent rebuke, and somehow persuade his pupils to enjoy poetry.

*To learn 'figures of speech'.* The fact that the pupil very quickly senses that the poet is more prodigal than the prose-writer in the use of literary contortions does not help him to love poetry. Why teach the pupil 'figures of speech' at all? Hyperbole and antithesis are habits of mind, and metaphor is a way of looking. When the pupil is advanced enough to appreciate this fact he can be taught his 'figures of speech'. If he is taught them before this he may never arrive at this crucial stage; and if the grammar book flaunts 'the Assyrian Wolf' too often, he will never come to like poetry, even if he understands its habits of mind.

*To teach grammar.* I am stating the worst cases first. Only a few teachers are quite so barbaric nowadays as to set a piece of verse for, say, clause analysis. Unhappily, many grammar books still follow this disgusting practice. To couple clause analysis, which is pretty nearly indefensible as an occupation for schoolchildren, with poetry is a very grave blunder.

*To teach scansion.* Scansion may come up in a poetry lesson. In a later chapter, I will give some good reasons why it should not be allowed to 'come up' very far or very often. To help a class discover the rhythm of a poem is one thing. To introduce a poem or poems so that they may be enabled to discover rules of scansion that apply to poetry in general is quite another. The scanner militant will find some observations on his pet subject in the chapter called *Examining*.

*To teach vocabulary.* This, like some of the other headings, can apply equally to literature in general. If someone wants to know the meaning of a word, obviously let him know it. There are certain ages, too, principally the primary ones, at which strangeness of vocabulary is an added excitement. For the most part, however, difficulties of vocabulary are annoyances, and one cannot afford annoyance in a poetry lesson. Vocabulary can be enlarged elsewhere, preferably indirectly.

*To teach history, etc.* Of course, there is no reason why history should not teach poetry. Sir John Moore can be buried quite gracefully after reading Napier's account of Corunna. Only, be careful.

*To teach the pupil 'a lesson'.* Some headmasters, only vaguely enlightened, insist that 'lines' should not be set as punishment because they are not constructive. Maths masters should make offenders write Pythagoras six times with different letters, etc. This sounds well, and invariably wins the approval of the parents; and since it makes little Johnny think, it is also ambitiously concluded that it is a more effective form of punishment. Alas: its effect on his maths is often damnable.

The temptation in English to make a slacker *learn* something by heart is strong. It should be resisted. Lines do have the merit of being divorced from the subject while remaining ingeniously married to the crime.

And lastly, and most regrettably, poetry is used to *teach the pupil poetry*. There exists at the back of one's mind when one is teaching the feeling that there are things that the pupil *ought* to know; it is, naturally, an educational primum mobile. Remember, in poetry, however, that if the pupil enjoys he will *want* to get to know. If you *make* him know he will only know as much as you make him (perhaps), and that process will stop on the day he walks through the front gate of the school with the headmaster's handshake of farewell his only pleasurable memory of the place.

Therefore, one's ideas of the 'grand pageant of English poetry', of chronologies, of presenting a number of pieces by one poet as a 'follow up', should go by the board. So also should the application to poetry of that most intelligent argument: 'he will get no more than he gets here; therefore it would be a crying shame if he did not read some Shakespeare, Shelley, etc. One day it will all come back to him and he will be grateful.'

To give pleasure should be the only aim in teaching the Arts; for they were conceived in order to give pleasure. If one's teaching of them omits pleasure, then one is in fact giving something false, something different. Shakespeare without pleasure is not Shakespeare.

All of these bogeys are obvious enough when one considers them in abstract; but while one is teaching they can quite easily creep in unnoticed.

Halfway through one's course with a particularly unresponsive form it becomes possible to will them in. Scansion, figures of speech, are satisfyingly tangible subjects. They have their own mystique and do much to restore one's self esteem. Nothing is better for one's ego when one is competing morally with factual subjects like the sciences (if one has a sense of 'competing' one is failing pretty miserably) nothing restores it so much as to thoroughly baffle a class.

All of this arises from a misconception. At no level, other than at university, should English be regarded as an academic subject. Like Art and Music, it is play. Approach it as play and, paradoxically, you will do more 'work' than if you treat it as 'work'. You will also draw energy and inspiration from the class. Reading literature is obviously play. Writing compositions can also be encouraged as play if they are the right kind of compositions. Alas: they very rarely are.

This brings us to a consideration of the teacher. When the aim is lost sight of the fault is undoubtedly in him; and yet, paradoxically, it is rarely his fault. As I have said elsewhere, it is difficult, in any 'pressure' education system, like that afforded by the grammar school or public school, to escape the idea that one's subject exists in competition with others. There is undoubtedly in many cases a pressure at staff level. The English teacher has an easy time: his is a woolly subject; and why is he mucking around with *Drake's Drum* when Smith major in form five still cannot punctuate his Chemistry notes properly?

In self-defence the English teacher becomes calligrapher, inspector of fountain pens, and principal detector of un-washed hands; and, worse still, he starts talking about things that an English master has no right to mention, like 'the real work involved' in his subject. This is nonsense.

Then he falls back on his one genuine grouse: his marking. Sitting at home this Christmas with nine hundred and forty pages of Sixth Form Essay lurking dismally beyond my anticipation of plum-pudding it was very easy to consign to perdition all of the Maths masters of the Universe. Their marking was done.

Reproach them with this fact, and they retort how jolly pleasant it is to read essays; and argue that English masters never read the things properly at any rate, and scarcely bother to correct what they read. The temptation to become a red devil, to incarnadine every syllable to oblivion, to be seen in the staff room late at night, meticulously writing in the correct answers, is very very great. It should be resisted.

I once marked heavily and meticulously. I now use the time getting to know what my pupils write. A child of any age is capable of producing memorable phrases, images, ideas. Commendation does far more for a pupil than any amount of red ink. To quote people's work to them gives them a fresh sense of its importance. Besides, shall I ever forget the little girl of six who wrote me a poem about The Wind, illustrated by a diagram of a daisy-eating quadruped against whose side stabbed a number of dotted lines seemingly bent in frustration, the text of which ended in the memorable statement:

> The wind blew over everywhere
> Till it was stopped by the side of the cow.

The age was six. The worthlessness of the rest of the poem did not matter. Education consists of praising the good not castigating the bad.

Pleasure is still the only aim. Try telling a form that it is a pleasure to work with them, that you enjoy reading their work. Try not correcting anything. Put a high mark at the bottom of the work and as fulsome a piece of flattery as you can dream up. Funnily enough, even the toughest of teenagers do not regard this sort of approach as soft. Stranger still, the mistakes that one spends hours correcting in other classes, and which are never eradicated, here quickly disappear.

In any event, in the teaching of English, and of poetry in particular, you achieve absolutely nothing by saying anything like 'this will not do'. If you do say it, you at once bring in the problem of academic progress.

Another hindrance when you set 'free' work (I will deal with this in the next chapter) is the fear that the child may 'crib' something. Certain boys and girls are able to produce quite remarkable pieces of writing, especially if they are invited to produce imaginative rather than essay-type compositions. There is a very great temptation to catechize them about possible 'sources'. To do so (and, after all, if you do not *know* it for a crib you are revealing to the person concerned a very grave personal insufficiency) is to completely mar any pleasure they take in the work if it is genuine, and quite certainly to shatter the bonds of mutual trust that are essential. For the record, only one of my pupils has ever 'written' a poem by an established poet.

Plagiarism, as distinct from direct transcription, is probably to be encouraged. Certainly any weaning from it must be gradual. In poetry composition it will not generally be noticeable until the late teens; and even then only in pupils who have been taught according to a different system.

The vocabulary of that last sentence indicates two of the remaining impediments to one's achieving the correct aim in the classroom (though I shall not modify my choice of words in the pages hereafter; like most schoolmasters I am enough of a bore without stooping to that sort of nonsense). The words that worry me are 'teach' and 'system'.

In English one does not teach so much as encourage.

In the 'teaching' of poetry almost everything depends upon the choice of material. It is hard to see what there is to 'teach'. Yet this is a matter in which many people require guidance; and in which the varying factors of personality are frequently ignored. There are sections of this book dealing with topics other than the 'choice of material'; but it is by this and almost by this alone that a teacher succeeds or fails in the first instance.

'Systems.' Other subjects have systems because, in many cases, like the sciences, for example, they are about systems. In 'teaching' the Arts there is really no system at all. One is concerned with the pupils' pleasure. Without pleasure there is no Art. It is the pupils' pleasure and not ours we are worried about; so our tactics are based upon our knowledge of our pupils and of what we can bring to them. What of Dryden's 'instruction'? What of the would-be wise words in Chapter I about the purpose of pleasure? That is strategy. Once in the classroom we are concerned with tactics.

There is perhaps one last general word. The biggest hindrances when one is trying to teach properly are one's 'travelling companions'. Anything that smacks of enlightenment in education is nearly always the special province of the crank, the inveterate sloth, or the poor disciplinarian.

To travel with the crank is as tolerable as to travel with the 'work-'em-hard-and-damn-the-pleasure' type. To abstain from red ink after carefully reading work and then to be grouped with the person who does not read the work is rather more annoying. About discipline, there is only one thing to say:

If you cannot command complete obedience from a class then there is no point in being a teacher. Methods may vary; but a man can give absolutely nothing, in spite of what the crank says, if he cannot keep order. The sort of order he keeps is up to him: some people allow talking while the class is performing certain exercises. Others do not. But unless the first group 'allow' rather than 'condone' they are grossly misleading themselves and their classes. In a school where standards of behaviour are not clearly set down and consistently adhered to teaching is a meaningless function.

One's total aim as a teacher is to encourage people to express themselves; not by throwing ink, however.

Discipline, by the way, is something quite apart from the

sort of teacher one is. Without it one can achieve nothing. With it, one may still achieve nothing. But there is a major heresy current at present, and that is that one's ability to keep order is directly proportional to one's ability to interest the class. That is nonsense: the bad disciplinarian can produce what would be a perfect lesson and it will not be heeded. He can ventriloquize, conjure, even set his hair on fire, and the class will not even look at him.

And why this digression? Because if you are going to teach the Arts, if you are going to interest people in poetry, which brings with it often (through no fault of its own) associations of effeminacy and fluff, then you cannot afford to be regarded as anything else but a competent and orderly citizen. To bring colour to children's lives is a noble aim. Yet it does not help to be the only member of staff who wears a lemon and pink waistcoat. Poetry must be represented as something capable of existing for the man at the bus-stop, the woman doing her shopping, for the adult the child is to become.

I am not proselytizing. I do not say that there are not ages at which posturing and the Arts go together. Indeed, there are moments in the child's development when it needs to identify itself with something that is 'different'. But the English master, of all men, should proceed carefully. Pleasure of the enduring kind is not communicated by the Outsider or Clown. The values discussed in the first part of this book must be upheld by ordinary men and women, or they will become meaningless.

# 4. MAKING

EARLIER I said that the best results are obtained in the teaching of English if it is treated as an Art rather than an academic subject. This is specially true of the teaching of poetry. One might go further and say that poetry can be approached in much the same way as Art itself.

Consider the Art teacher for a moment. His immediate aim is that his pupils should experience the pleasures of self-expression in line and colour. His more strategic aims, approximate to those discussed in the first section of this book, are that the pupil should increase these powers of self-expression, and that he should come to be more aware of Art in general and of Art in nature; in short, that he should gather more and more visual experience into himself.

Somewhere at the back of all English teaching exists the same idea of increasing experience and the ability to express experience in words. Art and English then, together with music, are especially central to education because they enlarge experience in a special direction: they deal with the problem of aesthetic awareness. The other subjects increase man's chance of living usefully and well: these help him to enjoy doing so.

Forgive me for simplifying propositions which have been made far more tellingly by other writers, and to which I have lent particular elaboration in Part One. Let us turn to the Art teacher again.

It is common ground that the ability to absorb experience is closely connected with the ability to express it. There is no such thing as a sealed man; if the power to communicate becomes atrophied so does the power to experience.

Children scribble early. They record visually the elongated adult world that towers above them with its inverted noses far sooner than they do verbally. Their verbal faculties are quickly enlarged by the oral practice of normal conversation, however; and by the age of ten they are already prisoners of their pencils far more than of their tongues. They are not yet prisoners of their pens, because their literary appreciation is still behind their visual. They can see by now that their drawings are hopelessly inadequate as an expression of life; they do not feel any literary inadequacy, because there is very little conscious correlation between their ability to talk and their ability to write, and quite certainly no sense of comparison between this latter and their appreciation of stories told in books.

Indeed, different mental processes are used for speaking sentences and for writing them, as one can often notice when reading a letter from an adult who in normal conversation has appeared most articulate. To the child of ten there is little very real frustration involved in efforts to write *unless* it is faced with the purely physical difficulty of producing something of a given length, say a letter of thanks to a relative, or of a greater degree of accuracy and tidiness than it is accustomed to. But the same child can be aware of its inability to draw a lifelike horse's head, and will even seek to remedy this defect by copying a technique of drawing, if a teacher is foolish enough to give an example. In other words, the child's artistic awareness is far in advance of its corresponding literary faculty.

I have discussed all this for the following reason, and it seems to me a good one. A great amount of educational research has been done to free the child from his artistic difficulties; and although the techniques concerned are not yet widely current they are at least being taught. No such research has been done on the teaching of English;[1] and consequently, when the child meets very similar difficulties in composition a year or two later, systems of the same flexibility are not available to overcome them.

At this stage there will be objections. Granted that what has been said rests upon a broad basis of fact, surely there is nothing therapeutic about the composition of poetry? And what has become of my earlier insistence on enjoyment? Surely the scarcely literate person finds himself even more imprisoned in the tower of verse. To this I can only reply that the processes I am about to describe will be demonstrated to be therapeutic (though this is not the main aim, for—yes—the pupils do enjoy them), that at certain ages—unbelievably, but I will illustrate this—pupils work better in verse than in prose, and are quite certainly better poets than prose-writers, and that the whole process bears out my remarks about poetry being central to education in practice as well as in theory.

For the moment, however, let us consider how the Art teacher is learning to overcome similar problems. At the focal point of this is the work being done by H. W. Sayer, who is typical of many Art teachers and the archetype of what is required but seldom found in the English teacher. Sayer is himself a meticulous draughtsman, trained at the Royal College of twenty years ago, and one of the most famous etchers in the country; yet with this tremendous personal bias towards precision he refuses to attempt to instil precision in others until, if ever, he judges them ripe for it. He is well aware of the fact that it would be fatal to confront a novice, whether child or adult, with problems demanding his own order of draughtsmanship.

Yet to learn is as to express as to express is as to progress.

[1] Most research in the teaching of English is aimed at encouraging the child *to receive* rather than *give.*

In Art the child must be conscious of a matching up of his powers with his experience or he will quickly become disheartened. What is needed is a medium which will make this possible. Mr. Sayer's answer is to begin with a large sloping paper, perhaps damp, on which areas of paint are placed and allowed to mix. Thus the child avoids the problem of transferring the image to a blank page. Nor initially does he have to look for the image: it is suggested by the mingling of the witching oils in front of him.

Once he has received this suggestion he is able to refine upon it until it is perfect, and so perfect does it often become, whether reality or fantasy, that it can resemble the work of a mature artist. Moreover, to this process of refinement can be brought all the devices of blotting paper, wax, fern, so that the pupil quickly has a grasp of the wide possibilities of the medium. Experience is directly proportional to expression. Here the pupil, of immature sensibility as yet, is able to find his experience in the paint, not seek to record a half-experience with implements over which he has imperfect control. Lest the process be felt a mere 'mucking about in paint' I would once again like to point out that the pupils produce paintings far in advance of their age-groups. It is one thing to set out to draw a horse; quite another to realize that a horse is happening, as it were, in front of one's eyes and to see that all it requires is encouragement. And strangely enough, one is far more likely to draw a horse after the second method has been experienced once than after weeks of undergoing the first.

'A mere mucking about with paint.' In fact, however, one does not seek much more of one's pupils in an English Composition lesson than that they enjoy mucking about with words. Or one should not.

The easiest way 'to muck about with words' is to write free verse, for here the child can be encouraged to enter a world of impressionism where the formal barriers of grammar and sequence are swept aside. The child's earliest teachings have in most cases been allied to grammar and sequence: here he is invited to explore the possibilities of association, and the results can be astounding. In many of the examples given later two trends will at once be obvious: first a tremendous fertility of invention; secondly a rationalizing of this power so that, judged even in prose terms, this work appears incredibly articulate. The child himself enjoys writing verse of this sort because it is simple and brings a quick liberation of ideas. With expression comes pleasure.

For the moment let us consider free verse itself. This has absolutely no meaning for a very young child at all; nor should it have. Infants for a time regard rhyme as a natural means of story-telling: they are not immediately aware of any difference between verse and prose; they merely prefer the former, and the more grotesque it is the better.

Once the difference between verse and prose is apparent there is often a strong tendency to prefer prose. Prose after all is the language of adventure stories. With clever teaching, however, verse can remain a particular source of enjoyment. There is scant excuse for losing a class's attention for poetry at any primary school age, except perhaps the last year.

It is already possible for free verse composition to come into its own. Rhymed verse is both difficult and undesirable as a written exercise for a youngish child who is not even very fluent in prose; but free verse is easy. It has, for the child, no rules, even less than prose—and for the moment the pupil can forget syntax and sequence and just play with words.

This, one suspects, does not even sound well in theory to those who have no knowledge of it in practice. How does one go about getting a class of ten-year-olds, say, to write verse?

One must assume that one's general poetry lessons are good. To harp incessantly on the obvious, this means that one's classes enjoy them, nothing more. Children of this age savour phrases rather than images, certainly rather than sentences. A condensed phrase, like a compound word, is especially pleasurable: snarleygob, callibonkers, gobstoppers, lickspit, anything extraordinary and contorted and preferably vulgarian enough to cause a mild stir when used as abuse.

They rarely get round to using these words in prose, other than in the sing-song prose of invective: they like poetry because it uses words of such gnarled appeal.

Invite them to play with this sort of word; let them build up lines, close in association, around something that they would like to describe. Dispense with rules, even the rules of prose, and present descriptive writing, of a thing, of a person, of one another, as the very happy game it is.

Later on, I shall include some examples of poetry written by this age group and the one just above it. It is the age of innocence, as these poems will show, and an age at which the child is willing to do anything requested of him—except nothing.

Therefore, one's basic technique need not be elaborate. One need say no more in the way of introduction than that the class is going to write poems, and then demolish quickly the rules by which poems are made. Poems are no more, one says, than people's ideas about something, jotted down in short lines as they come. Some rhyme, some don't. As an illustration I have never known this one fail:

> What a wonderful bird the frog are;
> When he sit he stand almost,
> When he hop he fly almost,
> And he ain't got a tail hardly, neither;
> That's all I want to say about the frog.

Please, the grammar is bad. Yes, I know. A very ordinary man wrote that, and now it's in all the books. (Nor does a grammatical letting down of hair lead to bad grammar, as I shall demonstrate later: quite the reverse.) For a young child, even the apparent freedom of this example presents dangerous difficulties, however. Once one *leaves* it with him, he becomes hampered by it. One must enable him to devise his own poem on the page in front of him, in a way comparable to the Art teaching method noticed above.

His problem, as in painting, resolves itself into two questions:

How do I start?

How do I carry on?

Help him to isolate his subject.

'What would you like to write about?'

'The carpenter.'

'What does he look like?'

'He's got a moustache, and—and one eye, and a bag of tools.'

Suggest that he heads the poem 'The Carpenter'; this gives him some capital; then tell him to put down the first word he thought of in connection with the carpenter:

'Moustache!'

What does it look like? The child may say, 'like my father's', 'like a moustache', or he may find a convincing image, or he may fall back on word attraction of the sort noticed earlier and say 'rhubarb' or 'sausage', he may recollect an adult phrase and say 'like a toothbrush', or with customary disregard for grammar, 'like the rats have been at it'. Embrace any of these ideas willingly. Or he may say nothing. In this case encourage the search for an image in the objects around him. The blackboard duster? the pot full of flowers? the fringe of the curtain? This approach need not be used with more than a few pupils, since the remainder of the class quickly take the idea. The more outrageous or humourous the suggestions the better.

In Particular

Eventually the poem may go something as follows:

> A moustache of thistle
> One eye like a bottle of ink
> And a bag of tools
> Like a banana full up with pins.

This is at best: and at best it will only be a first verse. At worst it is more likely to be:

> Moustache,
> One eye,
> A bag of tools
> Full of tools,
> Hammer,
> Chisel,
> Spanner,
> Some nuts.

In this case, suggest a rounding off line like 'Here comes the carpenter', and praise it nevertheless. A result so meagre will only be obtained from a pupil whose English is of a very low standard. As the examples given later will show, the general level of result is high.

The next stage is to enlarge the experience by working for coherence. After three lessons, during which you encourage single statements, the less able poem becomes something like this:[1]

> He has a moustache,
> I can see his one eye,
> And his large bag of tools
> Which is full of
> Hammers for knocking,

[1] I should emphasize that you never return to the same poem, or to the same subject. I use a similar example for convenience of exposition, merely.

54

*Making*

> Chisels for chipping
> And a spanner to tighten
> Some nuts.

This sort of statement is fairly representative of less able work, say a Primary B stream, age 9–10. I have not attempted to reproduce spelling, etc., but my remarks on this will be found later.

As anyone who knows this age and standard can see at a glance, the quality of this work, judged as prose, is high. The isolated thought unit has increased both in observation and coherence; and because each factor is so brief, and by itself on a line, one has been able to ask such questions as:
What does it look like?
What is it used for?
And, How does it fit into the general picture?
I have understated my case as the genuine examples given later will show. The teacher who has tried to develop coherence with less able pupils of this age will at once see its value as an exercise.

When I worked at a training college I managed to sell the idea of writing poetry to an elementary-school class that did not like reading poetry. The latter state of affairs can only arise as a result of gross incompetence with a class of this age, of course; but my success, also repeated with recalcitrant grammar-school classes, does not necessarily reflect any compensating competence. In each case I have been 'novus homo'. The new man will always be listened to (a fact which some training college lecturers and inspectors often ignore, when they hold a class's interest for ten minutes then look triumphant); but the moral to be drawn is that one must start as one means to go on. If one is to do new things with a class the second term is not the time, unless one wins their complete and progressive approval. The first term is best.

My method was to ask them whether they liked poetry. (One should never be frightened to face an honest opinion.) When they chorused 'no', I looked puzzled, and then asked them what poetry they had read. 'Oh that! I don't think very much of that myself. But that is not the only sort, you know.' Then I went on to talk about poetry that did not rhyme, that did not use fancy words; and said that this sort of poetry was as much fun to write as to read. They wrote.

The weak link in the argument, if you have to develop it, is that, with the exception of *The Frog*, and one or two others, there are no poems of this sort that will appeal to this age group other than those they write themselves—no unrhymed poems, that is. The important thing is to get them to write, and then praise, encourage, and help them improve. Anything they produce must be hailed as a poem (of sorts) and invested with reverence. The class very soon enjoys reading and listening to its own poems; I will elaborate the principles of development later.

Subjects are best left to them: their pets, their interests, etc. But if they do not easily find ideas (i.e. if they have been badly taught in the past) the following will serve as a rough area to work in:

Anything to do with animals,
> ghosts,
> unusual occupations like deep-sea diving, mining, train driving, etc., spacemen.

Exciting scenes like:
> Fire, Storm, Accident.

Places like:
> Hospital, the laboratory, etc.

One can give examples, but it is best to give only one. If not they will copy slavishly, and the whole exercise be ruined. It is far better to give unusual and suggestive images; if they are comic or grotesque, so much the better.

'Please, sir, I want to write about a fish.'

'A very good idea. A fried fish, a flat fish, or a queer fish? (Cheap verbal trade, but it pays off.)

'No, sir. A real fish.'

'Then write about the myrtle fish. It lives at the North Pole, and looks like a rhododendron leaf, and eats icicles.'

The wildly impossible image always succeeds, far more than any frigidly serious explanation. More than this, the class catch the idea of laughter.

With this age, English is fortunate in possessing supporting arms: the crayon, the paint pot, and the pencil; and one should encourage the drawing of the myrtle fish as well. It generally makes everyone feel better.

The child finds writing, compared to drawing, a bore. Writing progresses, according to unchangeable rules, in ruled lines across the page. It is to counteract its inflexible demands that one needs to introduce verse composition in the first place. E. E. Cummings's typographical nonsense in the poem about the mouse appears fun (not, I hasten to add, as *reading* material for this age; he is suitable merely as an introduction to typographical excursions in compositions), and great pleasure can be gained by playing with the appearance of words:

> the Gun *went* BANG.
> DOWN *fell* The man.

or

> The Gun went *
> The man said! ! ! !

A number of older pupils do not seem to be able to do without Block Capitals and asterisks. To meddle with this form of expression is wrong, even though in mature people it may represent various inadequacies. At a younger age, I think that pleasure is a sufficient justification for encouraging it, for pupils make progress in the subjects that please them. But other goods may come. An elementary school teacher said to me once when I was visiting his school that his pupils were making poor progress in punctuation, and showing little interest in any attempt on his part to teach them better. I suggested that they should be told, in quick general terms, about the history of punctuation, its difficulties, and its changes, and then invited to try to invent their own system in a different way. This resulted in several weeks' interesting work, and the conventional punctuation improved. Thinking about where their punctuation was needed helped them see where any punctuation would be needed. Besides, to set aside a rule for a moment is often the best way to discover its usefulness. A rule taught by rote is a bore.

Similarly with Apollinaire's

'My heart is like a flame turned upside down'

written in the shape of a heart; the poem on rain that straggles vertically down the page—these are good points of departure. One does not obtain outstanding work: but the class enjoys it. Pleasure can be invested in a subject like money in a bank. And it is a strange psychological truth that many of these sentences which do not keep to the railway track are better than those that do.

The techniques that have been mentioned, although new, will not have been vastly different from those employed by many teachers to facilitate their general work in composition. They are to some extent using verse composition to other ends than helping the pupil to enjoy poetry: nevertheless, they do help to keep poetry central to the curriculum at a time when it is in danger of being squeezed out by the eleven-plus.

## *Making*

In a recent census I conducted at a London grammar school it was found that some 30 per cent of the pupils had done no poetry at primary school. How stimulating the teaching of poetry at this age can be is seen from the fact that everyone who had read poems at primary school had enjoyed them. At this age, and at this age only, almost anything is better than nothing; for a number of pupils claimed to have enjoyed poems that one would have considered unsuitable, e.g. *The Ancient Mariner*, at the age of nine. Those pupils who had been encouraged to write verse, and they were few, preferred doing so. When they had been allowed to read their own poems to the rest of the class they had enjoyed this form of activity far more than reading poems by other authors. From what has been said before, this will appear only natural. One boy had been taught to write rhyming verse to quite a high degree of facility, and he expressed a clear preference for writing to reading. His prose composition, as one would expect, also followed a clear pattern of coherence and order; but he was deficient in any wider imaginative power. Unlike most eleven- and twelve-year-olds he could not be encouraged to think in images. Perhaps because of this formal training he was extremely uncritical of the poetic *status quo*. Once he accepted me as his English master. any poetry lesson, good, bad or indifferent, was an obvious pleasure to him, and he also (quite unique this, and certainly not a situation one would seek to encourage) liked every poem in a rather full, diverse, and not particularly distinguished anthology. His remarks on these poems were penetrating though generally concerned with their rhyme-scheme and metre and its relationship to the subject rather than to meaning, image, etc., but he seemed unable to establish any hierarchy of liking. In short, he had mastered something which was quite difficult, but only be-cause he had considerably more intelligence than his fellows, many of whom must have foundered. This difficult exercise, performed skilfully rather than instinctively, had limited him; he had not grown up with his skills. The whole point, while encouraging poetry composition, is to get the pupil to do what comes easily. Encourage as poetry what he has, not what one could want him to have. Free verse would have been better.

Well-taught or badly-taught, the first form at secondary school represents a fresh start. Still unhampered by puberty and pressure teaching their minds are eager to learn, or at least eager to please. The school teacher once more has the initiative. Let him begin at once and he can achieve anything. This is true of verse composition.

I shall give reasons later why verse composition is so beneficial to written and imaginative progress in general. For the present, the best reason for encouraging it is that the class can quickly be made to like it. In another chapter you will find my remarks on the uses and abuses of school anthologies. One is always in doubt about what will please. But, if the class writes, it writes what it wants to write. Properly encouraged a tremendous corporate spirit grows up in the first year. There are always ten people whose efforts when read aloud can be calculated to produce merriment, two more who will produce admiration. Providing everyone receives some praise from you and is allowed to read his own work he will be happy, no matter how weak initially. Pleasure begets pleasure, and thence comes progress. No matter how bad the first work is, tell them it is good. One thing you can be certain of for that first homework, and that is that the pupil has tried. However bad the work is it is someone's best. It should be encouraged.

It will be evident from what has been said that poetry composition could be regarded as a soft option, especially by the less able pupils. To attempt to eliminate the soft option is one of the pitfalls into which English teaching only too frequently blunders. If English as a whole is a soft option then people will enjoy doing it. A lot of the so-called 'poems' produced by less able pupils may only have taken them, say, a quarter of an hour to produce; but transcribe them as prose and the exercise, in terms of quality *and quantity*, will be found to have paid. Besides, one is asking for artistic endeavour, and a quarter of an hour, rather than a full homework period, seems a reasonable time over which to expect a young person to sustain such endeavour.

An additional point is that the mind is particularly prolific at this age—or, at least, while it is being exercised in a new way. Even on a quantitative basis (and heaven forbid that this should be considered over-important) a short period of time is adequate.

There are other virtues in this type of composition. May I bring them out by simple illustration. On p. 62 is a facsimile of a poem by a pupil whose prose work is most untidy. It will be seen from the quality of the manuscript that I am not picking an unfair example.

In the past I had received much untidy work from him. When I received this poem it was offered with an apology for its one erasure. Notice the vastly improved handwriting, the lack of error, and the sense, implicit in the long dashes and the layout, that a manuscript can be something to be treasured.

One recollects the pleasure when young that went into keeping any sort of notebook that had diagrams, ruled insets, subtitles, and lettered and numerated paragraphs, and of writing up subjects that called for three different sorts of ink and a plentiful use of crayon. English composition cannot generally offer such enticements: here is one field where its inducements are at least of an equal nature. The linking of verse composition and Art at the beginning of the chapter is not an arbitrary association.

# SCHOOL.

1. Oooh! — isn't it horrid,
   Oooh! — isn't it bad,
   Oooh! — this was the death, I expect,
   Of some poor little lad.

2. Oooh! — what a sight,
   Oooh! — what a place,
   Oooh! — isn't it frightening when you
   ~~you~~ see a master's face.

3. Oooh! — isn't it eery,
   Oooh! — doesn't it reek,
   Oooh! — you're likely to die here
   Inside of one week.

4. Oooh! — isn't it haunted,
   Oooh! — it's like a spook,
   Oooh! — it filled me with terror,
   At every step I took.

Such a manuscript should be treated with the reverence it deserves: it is not to be butchered with red ink. Nor is it to be impounded as an example. Ask the author for a copy, and he will generally be happy to provide one even more magnificent.

Indeed, this gives rise to a further technique. The classroom should not be the end of this poetry. Whenever possible pupils should be encouraged by having work printed in the school magazine: it provides an extra, though inadequate platform; a form magazine is even better, as it intensifies the work's appeal to the collective audience, which is both an appreciative and a critical one, because it has participated in the poem's first birth.

I keep a file of my classes' work, and this means that I can select work which the school and form editors have rejected. It is also a symbol of my own interest; and two or three times a week someone turns up with an unsolicited poem for the form file.

The presentation of poetry becomes, as I have said, synonymous with taking care. In this way, as well as stimulating a feel for words and being an uninhibiting medium for image, it encourages the elimination of basic grammatical error. Consider this piece of prose:

Lord Avery*s* mistake

Lord *a*very drove along in his decrep*id austain*. A bum*b* knocked *of* a door. Alknock R*d* kept running through his mind. Alknock was *thee most* posh place in London.

Lord Avery had almost forgotten that he was a peer *to the relam, as shown in* his car and clothes and.of course/money. . . . If Al(Lord A) had any sense he would have *relized* that it couldn't mean the posh Alknock, but/there/he hadn't any brains.

*In Particular*

And these pieces of verse:

BIRDS

Oh how I wish I *was* a bird,
Free to all obligations,
To roam, to fly
Free to myself,
To soar unaided,
by no motion powered,
Oh how I wish I was a bird.

Oh how I wish I was a bird.
Their wings flash,
Their beaks are bright
And their plumage glorious.
No man could stop me.
Oh how I wish I was a bird.

THE SUN

That ball of gleaming fire,
Powerful, mighty beyond all things!
It gives us light and health
Shinning on us down below.

When it goes every night,
Fear clutches every man below.
In the morning, bright again,
Gay thoughts to each man it gives.

These pieces, prose and verse, are all by the same boy, and
were all submitted together. They were all free activity; that
is they were unsolicited contributions for the school maga-
zine. In a 'set' composition the boy's prose standard falls far
below this example.

Two things emerge: although the prose is powerful it is full of error, whereas the poetry is not. The prose shows nothing of the sensitivity of the first, quite remarkable, poem. The sense of rhythm and vocabulary displayed by the poem, the sheer intoxication, are qualities that can be enlarged, and which will enlarge the boy's composition in general.

He is an average grammar school pupil. He is eleven years old.

Before going further I would like to include some examples of work by children of ten, eleven, and twelve years of age. I am including them largely because they are good, and because they will therefore be, to some extent, propaganda for this method. It should be emphasized that these poems have not been widely gleaned: they were all produced by the same small group of boys. There are many others in the group equally talented. My only method was to suggest the pleasure of writing poetry, and to follow up its practice with such other techniques as will appear. Their enjoyment is evident in every poem.

## GROUP A

This first group is the result of a simple and straightforward approach, undertaken soon after I had met the form:

'This is a school where we enjoy poetry by making it together. We can forget rhyme for a minute, and concentrate on expressing our thoughts.'

Included among this section are poems written later, after I had developed the idea of the visual image; and of the aural image. My method was merely to start with the object, and ask for a comparison. Of these, K. Ash's poem on the train seems to me the best. In one or two poems the poets have employed a refrain. I did not suggest this, but praised it when it first appeared.

One poem is given as an example of the sort of work

achieved when one asks the class to talk about their present situation. It seems to me an unenterprising approach; and I am glad I did no real damage.

Some of the poems, e.g. those about the Prison, are 'image inspired' poems, rather than 'image association' poems. I spoke to the class of the many exciting things to describe near the school: the hospital, the prison, the White City, Shepherd's Bush Market, the Television Studios, and so on; and I built up quick image pictures of these. Interestingly enough, the class almost universally rejected my images and supplied their own. This was highly significant; the great danger is that they will slavishly copy an example. Hence the studied intangibility of the methods I have suggested.

N.B. Some boys wrote rhyming verse at once. I did not stop them. They were my introduction to later lessons.

### TRAINS

Trains are snorting monsters,
Running on snaky railway lines.

An express train at night is like a jewelled snake,
Writhing round the curves in the track.

A goods train is like a line of dirty men,
Plodding home after a hard day's work.

But I like trains.

K. ASH

### THE SALMON

The urge—
The call—
Of the sea.
The parr,

*Making*

Young salmon,
Sweeping
To the sea.

Multitudes,
Of young fish,
Being hurled
O'er the rocks,
Some to their death—
On the rocks.

The sea!
Yes the sea!
Is in sight,
Like a sheet—
A great sheet,
Of rippling,
Rippling rubber.

The life of the salmon
Goes well in the sea.
So back up the river,
They go,
But now they are huge—
And lords of the water—
The salmon—freshwater king.

### FISH

A piscine fin—
A piscine tail—
Waving,
Peacefully,
Placidly,
Fish

*In Particular*

Leviathians of the deep.
Drift gently past,
Going on their way,
Peacefully,
Placidly,
Going on their way
Like kites,
Submerged deep,
Peacefully,
Placidly,
Fish. . . .

BRIAN M. SHARPE

### AFRICA

Africa is like a galaxy of stars.
There are forests, deserts, jungles,
Arab, headhunters, tribesmen,
Missionaries, witchdoctors and more.
Africa is a dark place.
It is large dangerous and fierce.
Swamps that drown you,
Rivers like seas,
And jungles like hell.
It is still unexplored.
The snakes lions and other animals.
The lions that kill you,
The snakes poison you.
Yes it is a dark place indeed.
Men have died of horrible diseases,
Typhoid, malaria and other things as bad.
Men have gone there never to return.
I would not go there,
I wish to live not die.

BERNARD HOLLEY

# Making

## CATS

Cats,
Are like a ball of wool, rolling down a hillside,
When cats are at play,
You feel as if a lion is chasing you
Through a paradise of tables and chairs.

Cats,
When angry, are like a dragon,
Burning you with his fiery tongue;
But if you fight back:
It pangs your heart,
For you love the creature really.

A BARNARD

## A PRISON

A prison is like a great gaunt castle,
With great big walls and doors
Studded with spikes,
As if to keep a herd of elephants inside,
But only men are there.

Inside are great long passages,
With cells on either side.
Long, dark and spooky,
With warders pacing them up and down,
To see that no man escapes.

But even with great big walls and doors,
And all the precautions of guards and warders
Men still escape,
And slip over the great big wall like
December spooks,
But they are brought back.

K. ASH

*In Particular*

### HARVEST

In autumn the farm is all in a flurry,
As the corn is gathered in.
Lines of sheaves all standing in a row,
Like the soldiers being inspected
By their commanding officer.

Men running about picking up sheaves,
Like ants hurrying on their way,
Taking food to their nests,
Then the men go to the threshers,
To the threshers thumping and bumping.

Out come bales of hay,
No more ears are there,
But instead there is flour,
Soft and white and ever so fine
Going in sacks like silver snow.

TERENCE HEATHER

### THE SKY

The sky is like an endless mystery,
Flecked with white and blue,
The stars and planets
Are all in this far away abode.

The aeroplanes explore it,
Go far and wide,
But they cannot find
The wondrous, indescribable thing
That makes it all.

There are explanations
Of this unknown thing.

## *Making*

It is like a vast field of blue,
With white sheaves of corn
Spotted o'er.

H. FAIRWEATHER

### THE TEMPEST

For days the air had been still and ominous,
As if brooding upon an impending storm.
Suddenly, the silence was shattered
By a cataclysm of sound.

The vast panorama of water was rent asunder,
Fantastic billows shook the cliffs.
The reverberating roar echoed around
The many caves along the sea-shore.

How, out of the abysmal depths of the sea,
This hurricane force was being pumped
Is a mystery as old as time,
A mystery ne'er solved, ne'er explained.

H. FAIRWEATHER

### THE SACK OF TROY

The city blazes,
Stone walls crack and crumble
Like new bread before a blunt knife.
Trojans fled through black streets fringed with living,
moving red,
Like the great mosaic of a huge jigsaw puzzle.
They are pursued by warlike Greeks
With helmets, armour and shields of burnished brass,
With spears of sharpest iron and horsehair plumes.
Just within the city's walls rests the Wooden Horse,
Doom of the house of Priam of Troy,

71

*In Particular*

Hiding place of the incendiaries.
Avenging Greeks fling flaming brands
On houses not as yet ignited.
The acrid, greyish smoke can be seen for miles
Rising in swirling arabesques above the city.
Great rifts appear in Priam's palace walls,
Which collapsed 'mid showers of sparks and lambent
flames.
The blood-red luminous glow is seen for miles,
And at dusk appears as another sun,
Outshining by far the pale, waning moon.
And for days after the inferno's beginning the lucent
embers smoulder.

D. PHELPS

THE WIND

The wind,
It is a ghostly hand
Pushing to and fro,
The leaves and stray paper
That lay scattered in his path.

The trees
Bow down to the strength
Of the whistling wind,
As though paying homage
To some unknown king.

N. CAREY

## GROUP B

This group of poems is the result of giving the boys a list
of words and asking them to use them, or as many as possible,
in a poem.

## *Making*

N.B. This is not just a word exercise. The words
must be chosen because they belong together and
because they stimulate imagination.

The words I suggested in this instance are obvious. I also
suggest groups of shorter, less ornamental words, like 'filch',
'smirch', 'swag', 'grog', 'smog', 'smoke', 'grime', 'leer', etc.
About ten words are enough.

A colleague of mine actually gives a simple 'free' pattern to
his classes, as well as a vocabulary. Something like:

> 'I saw the sea
> Looking like . . .
> Or . . .
> (Verb) towards the shore'.

I must concede his results are good; but I feel my own
method is stereotyped enough, possibly too much so; though
the reader can judge this. I think that to limit the imagination
by imposing a pattern, when one's whole object is to enable
the child to discover a pattern, is quite wrong.

In the poems offered, there is another point to notice.
Although writing about a fire, the pupils do not let them-
selves be bewildered by such a generic title always. One
writes about 'The End of the Petroleum Warehouse'.
Another completely rejects the list of words, yet produces a
remarkably good poem. It would have been stupid to
reprimand him.

### THE FIRE

The fire glows
It certainly goes
Like a great big bomb
It licks the sky
And he who goes near it shall die.

## *In Particular*

The area is illuminated
And the house is ill-fated
For it looks like a skeleton
Away from it all shy
And he who goes near it shall die.

The fire is extinguished
And the remains are charred
And the skeleton collapses
'Oh well' does the owner sigh
'All who went near it did die.'

WILLIAM MARTIN


### THE BONFIRE

The bonfire
Fierce and incandescent
Is like
An inferno, blazing.

The smoke
Rising in arabesques
Makes ever changing mosaics
In the evening sky.

The acrid fumes
Overpowering and choking
Have no mercy
On those in its way.

The bonfire
When nearly extinguished
Has still
Lambent flames in the luminous embers.

(Unsigned)

## *Making*

### THE END OF THE PETROLEUM WAREHOUSE

The night was very dark and drear,
Midnight was creeping extremely near;
When suddenly with a tremendous explosion,
An inferno appeared and caused a commotion.

The sky then was glowing,
As petroleum was flowing
Lambent and lucent from a mosaic of burning wood.

Minutes later fire engines were rushing,
As flames and smoke from the warehouse were
    gushing;
Men and women and children were racing,
As the burning Petrol a path was tracing.

Soon lucent embers were sprawled around,
Upon the desolate fire-charred ground,
Six hours later all that was left
Was a mosaic of embers strewn adrift.

R. NICKLEN

### THE FIRE

'Look out!' yelled the firemen
'It's a-coming down.'
'Look out!' gasped the crowd that was ranged around.
The blazing inferno, that once was a house,
Now eaten with fire, like a cat eats a mouse,
The heat was intense, and the air was thick,
The inmates were rescued, but the house was a stick.

Poor old thing, she once was so proud,
Of beautiful structure, and nose in the cloud,

And from the grounds, to the turrets, where the doves
    were a–coo-in',
A misguided flame had brought it to ruin.

MICHAEL GOULDSBOROUGH

## GROUP C

These are mainly rhyming poems. I did not teach rhyme:
it is an unteachable activity. They had the example of their
fellows, of my own efforts to write with them, and of their
anthologies, to guide them.

Rhyme, like the attempt of the child to draw a horse
noticed earlier, ultimately brings frustration. I develop it only
to abandon the single poem for the techniques I shall describe
next.

### THE MAN IN THE MOON

The man in the moon,
Is coming soon,
    In his very fast car,
And when we try to catch him,
    He laughs, ha! ha!

His car can go a 1,000 an hour,
No wonder that we all cower,
    Here he comes, there he goes,
My golly, is he going fast,
    Ah, good, he's gone at last.

DEREK SNEESBY

### THE DREAM

The other night I had a dream,
I think it was of school.
I dreamt that it was maths, and I,
Forgot to bring my rule.

## *Making*

And then, to my dismay, I found
My compass had gone.
The master looked me in the eye,
And said, 'O silly John!'

'Into the corner, my dear boy,
And stand upon your head
And you will stay there all the day,
Till you simplify  x squared z.'

And so I stayed there all the day,
Standing upon my head,
But, when I woke up suddenly,
Oh! I found I was in my bed.

J. ADAMS

### CRICKET

I like to watch a game of cricket,
  As on the grass I lie.
The batsman hits the ball towards me,
But I see the ball flash by.

'Good old Peter,' the crowd all shout,
'He's scored another four,
Which brings his total to seventy-one.'
For that's what the crowd all roar.

The crowd soon moan, for very next ball
Old Peter's given out.
'Put your spectacles on, umpire, and look,'
For that is what the crowd shout.

C. ROGERS

*In Particular*

THE INVISIBLE MAN

He pops up here.
He pops up there.
He pops up everywhere.

He is the invisible man.
Try and find him, if you can,
If you can, if you can.

Where he is you do not know,
He! He! He! Ho! Ho! Ho!

Like a block of nothing walking about,
He'll swallow you up if he can.
Beware! Beware!! BEWARE!! BEWARE!!
Beware, the invisible man.

A. BARNARD

SUPERSTITIONS

Get out of bed with your right foot first.
Ladders you must *not* walk under.
If you do such things you will get bad luck.
A stupid and foolish blunder.

Look in your cup at the tea-leaves,
Make sure that the pattern's alright,
Or you may come home and find that your house
Has been 'Broken and Entered' that night.

Don't bring hawthorn into the house,
For that is bad luck again.
Look for black cats wherever you go
Or you *might* get a bad stomach pain.

## *Making*

Look at the stars in the sky every night,
Your astrologer see every day
'Phone up a Witch Doctor three times a week
Or your skies will appear very grey.

Don't let robins into the house,
(That means someone will die)
And don't you grumble about your bad luck,
You'll get good luck by and by.

D. PHELPS

'They Were; They Are; And They Will Be.'

Fred was a tubby fellow he was,
    Always jolly, and stupid he was,
One day when going for a walk, he was
    Surprised to meet his friend he was.

His friend was very small he was,
    Always cursing and swearing he was,
The secretary of the bank he was,
    But don't forget I said, 'He was'.

Fred is now tall and skinny he is,
    He's always sad and learned he is,
On days when he's going for a walk, he is
    Never surprised to meet his friend he is.

His friend is now very big he is,
    He's always preaching a sermon he is,
The husband of a banker's daughter he is,
    But don't forget I said, 'He is'.

*In Particular*

Fred will be rich and noble he will,
    He'll always be proud and clever he will,
When going for a walk, he will
    Be ignorant of his friend he will.

His friend will be poor and lowly he will,
    He'll always be begging and gambling he will,
He'll be head of the Poor Man's League he will,
    And this is the end of my story called
'They Were; They Are; And They Will Be.'

R. NICKLEN

GANGSTER WARFARE

My friend and I were prowling,
Prowling in the dark,
When we were asked what we were doing
We answered 'Just 'avin' a lark'.

We were really going to attack,
Attack our rivals' lair,
But when we got to their creepy place,
We thought they weren't there.

Then came a screech, a squawk,
A crash, a bang, a thud,
Then came the rival gangster's voice
'Reach for the celing, Bud'.

But then we heard the tramp of feet,
'Get out of here you four'
Said he 'We're surrounded by grown-ups',
We all dashed through the door.

And that did end our escapade,
And I didn't ask for more,

## *Making*

When father slapped me right and left,
I still feel very sore!

A. GOLDING

### A TALE OF TWO CATS

I have two cats
Named Splash and Whisky
Who in the evening
Are very frisky.

One taps the other
On the nose
Eventually
They come to blows.

Whisky goes
For Splash's tail
Splash turns round
And makes him fail.

Of this they soon
Begin to tire
They call it quits
And they retire.

(Unsigned)

### THE TRAIN

Past the Rock of Gibraltar
The train's speed did not alter,
It covered the trees in smoke
Some overhanging branches broke.

The anxious waiting porter
Talking to a sly reporter

G        81

*In Particular*

Reported: 'The train is very late.'
And then it came past
Not travelling very fast.

As the train drew by the porter's side
He sighed in exultation;
The reporter only said:
'There's no sensation.'

B. GRIEFF

Such composition cannot be indulged in for ever. If it could grow up as rapidly as critical promise often leads one to believe, then one could reasonably expect every grammar school class to possess, by the sixth year, its own Shakespeare and its own Wordsworth and Milton.

Fan it how you will, and fan it you must, this early flame of image association soon burns out. Puberty, in boys, seems to leave them with a curious deadness of invention; and when a fuller intellectual vigour returns to them they are often new people imaginatively. The bright images have been extinguished. They look for wit and for violence in literature and this desire cannot be met by the composition of single poems.

Girls have a similar problem; and though in their case these do not seem to militate directly against the prospects of successful teaching, the lack of imaginative freshness still becomes apparent. Not to make progress is not to enjoy.

No, at best this sort of composition is only a one-year device; and, I must hasten to insist, it is only for this year. With eleven-year-olds, at a new school, it is a marked success. Introduced for the first time to twelve-year-olds success is less certain. With thirteen-year-olds it is almost sure to fail.

A new technique must be used, started perhaps in the first

year and used more insistently in the second when interest in the former composition starts to flag.

One needs to apply the composition of verse to something else, preferably drama. A rhyming verse play can be ready for performance with one period's preparation, and one period's (or one homework's) writing on the part of the whole class. I know of no other school activity which can so quickly bring so much enjoyment, and at the same time advance the pupils' powers of composition.

The simplest way of going about it is as follows: Propose the idea to the class (they never fail to respond because (a) it is better than a conventional composition, (b) they are writing something with a part for all of them, (c) they will have a chance to exhibit themselves and be laughed at).

Ask them for a subject.

In the first stage, quickly, orally, make up a plot yourself, the more unlikely and picaresque the better, and allocate each pupil one episode. Characters will come to mind as the plot burgeons. Only the major characters will come into more than one scene, so there are no real problems of character continuance. Remember you want to find perhaps thirty-six characters. (Make a note of the names as they are invented.)

The more riotous your own imagination is at this stage the better. Don't do too much thinking for them, but give quick suggestive images to promote their interest.

Then allow them about fifteen minutes for consultation with their neighbours, rough paper in hand, so that there will be no bad overlaps. At this time, move around, offering advice and adding fuel generally.

Here is an example of one that went well, as nearly as I can recall.

'Sir, what about a pantomime?'

'No, sir, what about space-travel?'

*Self:* Let's do both. How about 'Jack and the Space Stalk'?
(Pretty general approval, but strike while the iron is hot. If you pause there will be thirty-four more suggestions and an increasing unwillingness to do someone else's idea.)
Right, 'A'; you will scriptwrite Scene One. 'Jack Sent to Market'. Scene opens, Jack in bed with the prize pig. Mother wakes him up with his early morning cup of firewater. Jack spits out the counterpane, takes the pig's trotters out of his eyes, brushes his nose, wipes his teeth, unbuckles the grass-snake that is holding up his pyjamas, shakes the snails from his boots, unties his fingers, and rubs himself down with nettles. While breakfasting he is told by his mother to go to market.
'B'—Scene Two! You will need a narrator. 'Jack on the way to market', to buy the pig some artificial teeth. How does he know what size? The pig's bitten him, and he's to get some to fit the bite. How could the pig bite him if it had no teeth? 'She', Smith, if you don't mind: it was a lady pig. The teeth came off in the wound, if you must know. No, he was bitten on the elbow. Why did the pig want some more teeth? She was courting. No, I don't know whether pigs have teeth. Ask your dentist.
Right, 'C', Jack and the Double-Cross-Eyed Gypsy (he was wearing spectacles).
*C:* Gypsies don't wear spectacles, sir.
*Self:* I said he was a twister. Gypsy persuades Jack into parting with all of his mother's money in return for the seven space beans.
*C:* What are space beans, sir?
*Self:* The indigestive variety. They glow in the dark like canteen custard, and they born a hole in your pocket like the money you buy them with.
*C:* What about the pig's teeth, sir?

*Making*

*Self:* The lady pig's teeth, 'C'! Don't be greedy. That's 'D's' episode.

And so on. Jack goes home, gets scolded by his mother who throws the beans out of his window, and is sent to sleep in the hay without his winkle supper while the sow sleeps in his bed.

During the night the beans take root and the next morning Jack sees the space-stalk towering outside. Taking his scout knife, a pocketful of marbles, and the latest copy of the *Eagle Comic*, he mounts until, nestling in the topmost boughs he comes across a space-ship. He steps inside and—hey presto!—he's off.

On the flight he bores through a hollow star, nearly collides with the sun, fights off a fleet of phantom space-invaders, and, worse still, becomes aware of the space-ship's celestial crew: Junk the Jitter man, Bosco the Disembodied Brain, and Orc the Anthropoid Octopus. But he is protected by the stellar influences of Wily, the lucky winkle, who, once in outer space, comes unexpectedly to life in his pocket.

They land on the moon, get involved in incredible adventures with carnivorous shrubs, closing caves, one-eyed monsters, hound-dogs, hawk-eyed schoolmaster birds, creeping treacle, and the Tappercombs, ten-ton gorgons whose presence spells putrefying death.

Most amazing are the moon beetles who hoard and guard pebbles of uranium 263; Jack vanquishes these by imitating Johnny Ray, and returns to earth with his pockets loaded with uranium.

Back at the cottage, Jack buys his mother a washing machine and the sow a television set. The uranium earns him an immediate knighthood and honorary professorships galore, so he no longer needs to go to school.

'What protected him from radiation, sir?'

'The fact that he could sing like Johnny Ray.'

With a keen, responsive form I find I can think ideas up very quickly. They are probably tame enough in cold print; but they keep the class amused and happy, and better than that they stimulate a form of linguistic and imaginative thinking that cannot be otherwise than beneficial. One appreciates that not everyone can work this way, though it is surprising how well the mind functions before a young form which sets up no pressures. If spontaneity is impossible then obviously a little preparation will achieve the same result.

I find boys of this age more inventive with humorous plots, even in prose, and even in ordinary narrative serials. When writing rhyming verse drama, they are aided in humorous composition by the undoubtedly pantomimic effect of bad rhyme, and correspondingly hampered in serious composition.

What is achieved by all this?

Well, one can be certain the class enjoys it immensely. Composition, dramatic expression are vastly boosted; criticism is very active in a group effort of this sort since the class learns from its own mistakes without their having to be instructed. The most important thing, however, is that one is increasingly cementing the union between pleasure and poetry. This is a valid aim in itself. Weigh its other advantages, and I believe its claim to be considered as an essential activity is unanswerable.

People often ask where one gets the class-time for this sort of composition. I should explain that the techniques employed above represent nearly a half of the time one would spend upon composition in general. The remainder of the time is spent on compositions that, although not properly within the scope of this book, are complementary to the methods which are.

*Making*

In negative terms: I do not waste a class's time and dissipate their interest by asking them to write essays. An essay is a dead art-form; and its approach to life is not the approach of a child of 11, 12, 13, or 14: it analyses and he wishes to narrate. For what it is worth I *have* taught in a school that expresses its entire composition programme as follows: term one—the narrative paragraph; term two—the descriptive paragraph; term three—the argumentative paragraph; leading logically—oh bliss!—at the beginning of the second year to that most enjoyable experience—the Essay. One could hardly pursue boredom with more determination.

How does the pupil fare in an exam-conscious school—say a grammar school—as a result of not being taught the essay, and yet being expected to write essays in terminal and G.C.E. exams?

The answer is 'very well'. These methods aid the pupils in composition because they are being exercised in a broad and lively fashion. The exam essay, never practised beforehand for the terminal exam, but merely explained, is justified as the best method the examiner has for testing *all* of the skills they have enjoyed acquiring. I go on to point out that their performances in poetry and drama and short-story composition vary according to mood; but that most people are less temperamental when writing an essay. Besides, they would not like to be told to write a poem or a story on a given subject; but if the examiner does not give the subject how does he know it has not been prepared in advance?

When they need to know how to write an exam answer for, say, English Literature in the G.C.E. the essay becomes immediately justifiable as a means of expressing ideas, and their standard is always higher, both because the essay does not bring stale convictions, and because all of their compositional faculties have been exercised in the past by far, far better methods. One need have no fear, even from a grammar school point of view, of sacrificing the essay in order to gain time for the composition under consideration. Another advantage of this type of composition is that it continues to grow. Critical and creative processes keep it in a state of flux as it progresses from first reading to—if there is time—a rehearsed class performance. Words are changed, fragments are written in, and others written out. The group takes over the inspiration of the individual and modifies it, or suggests to the individual that he should modify it himself. This is far better than formal correction.

Besides, the whole business of preparing and editing a final script and then rehearsing it calls into play a more complicated set of pleasure associations. It is a process worthwhile for the sake of poetry and pleasure, but worthwhile for other reasons as well. The form wants to act at this age, but it would far rather act its own play; and, of course, the fact that it is its own play means that it is the right sort of play.

Something else emerges. The pupil-teacher relationship, tend it how you will, cherish it as sensitively as you can, still resolves itself into a simple matter of submission of material, and return with praise or correction. It is an artificial relationship creatively, and although a following up of the systems I advocate in the chapter on Method will do much to disguise its artificiality, they cannot alter it. After a time the pupil's mind becomes immune to praise or blame from a teacher; immune, of course, to blame more quickly than praise. But it is never immune to the reactions of fellow pupils. In repetitive compositions there comes a point where old, corrected, mistakes start to reappear; by using non-repetitive methods, assuming one has wit and invention enough, one can ameliorate this tendency—but not alter it. Pupils make few mistakes, other than those which proceed directly from ignorance, when they are writing a script to be read by their fellows, on the other hand. This is valuable in that it induces correct habits of mind and a correct sense of care; and more in that it indicates to the teacher the real errors, the ones to which he can most profitably turn his attention.

Two more goods accrue as a result of the pupil's preparing work for a pupil audience. One is that, as an extension of the first, the pupil will often be at pains to find out for himself what is a correct usage. The second, and you will see how this second-year system continues in its own way so many advantages of the first, is that he will write neatly if his script is to be used as an acting copy by his fellows. One 'Excuse me, sir, but I can't read his writing', in the middle of the big scene is worth ten times more than any amount of preaching or punishment that one can inflict oneself.

In a sense, this method is the key to all future work in verse composition until one is dealing with people of sixteen years old or over. Applied verse, the chance to write a rhyming pantomime, comic episode, 'Goon-show', school skit, will always go down well.

With older classes, one must be content with less, unless one has been lucky enough to teach them earlier as well. If one is broaching the subject for the first time with a class of fifteen- or sixteen-year-olds, it is necessary to establish oneself as the script-writer and edit every couplet as it is composed. Then the whole thing becomes a sort of elaborate *bouts-rimés.*

What one achieves, however, is something that is no less valuable, though it may be shorter. The verse is more sophisticated; one creates with the class, and therefore one's criticism is creative and unobtrusive; and the finished product is no less enjoyable to perform together and no less stimulating verbally. When one considers the shortage of pleasure-giving verse and drama for this age-group, there is much to recommend the celebration of the following sort of writing:

*Cinders:*      O, O, O,

## In Particular

You promised I could go.
Alas! Alack! O what a bore
To have to kneel and scrub the floor;
I have to wait, and dilly-dally
While Bert is jiving at the Palais.
My dress is dirty. What shall I do?
I can't afford one that is new.
Help: here come those beastly hags—
Dressed up posh, while I'm in rags.

*Narrator:* The wicked sisters enter 'Right'
While Cinders looks, recoils in fright.

*1st Sister:* Gerty's bust 'er last suspender.
Cinders, 'ave you one to lend 'er?

*Cinders:* Alas! I have not one to lend her.
I too have lost my own suspender.

*2nd Sister:* You aint no blasted good to us.
Look what washing kitchens does.
Fold up your duster and forget your soul.
What you need is rock and roll.

*1st Sister:* Come on, Gert, let's leave this dive.
Go on out and have a jive.

*Cinders:* But what of me, stuck in this hole?
What chance have I to rock and roll?

*2nd Sister:* Come with us.

*1st Sister:* Not on your nelly!
Let her stay and watch the telly.

*Cinders:* That idea's completely gone,
There's only 'Prudence Kitten' on.
O, dear sisters, let me go.
Tommy Steele, he sends me so.

*1st Sister:* Look at her in all those rags.
Come on, Gerty; where's the fags?

*2nd Sister:* She's really fed up. I can tell it.

*1st Sister:* Her face is her fortune. Let her sell it.

# Making

|  |  |
|---|---|
| *2nd Sister:* | Let's not now sit here and scoff. |
| | Grab the cash and let's push off. |
| | Her clothes are bad; her figure's grim. |
| | Let's go jive with Bert and Jim. |
| *1st Sister:* | Let's leave her here to sit and mope. |
| | With clothes like that she's got no hope. |
| | So let's away and start to creep, |
| | While she crawls into bed to sleep. |
| *Narrator:* | Exit sisters on the 'Left', |
| | While Cinders sits at home, bereft. |
| *Cinders:* | The Telly's here for bad or good. |
| | Perhaps I'll find it's Robin Hood. |
| | O dear! Now I've switched it on, |
| | It's only Lonnie Donegan. |
| | O this is sickening for me. |
| | Switch over quick to I.T.V. |
| | I'd rather romp with Friar Tuck, |
| | Than listen to that sort of muck! |
| *Narrator:* | She watched, but only half awake, |
| | Until there came a natural break. |
| *Announcer:* | Ladies, you know where you are |
| | When you wear . . . |
| *Cinders:* | My granny's bra!— |
| | It's fallen on the kitchen fire. |
| *Announcer:* | Of it's support you'll never tire! |
| *Cinders:* | But granny will. |
| *Announcer:* | Wait till she sees |
| | This latest line of 'Liberties'. |
| *Cinders:* | That's only for the upper crust. |
| | It cannot help poor granny's bust. |
| *Announcer:* | Girls! Give your hair that extra coil. |
| | Use Esso-Visco-Static oil. |
| *Cinders:* | I have to keep my ringlets clean |
| | With grandma's pot of vaseline. |

## In Particular

*Announcer:* O ma! O me! O my! O mo!
Just watch those dirty patches go!
Now you'll see, before your eyes,
Who's won the special Omo prize.
We've judged whose washing seems the best
According to 'the window test'—
Miss Mary Smith of Cheam.

*Cinders:*                                         O brother!
That's my fairy Godmother!

*Announcer:* Now listen to her special tip.

*F. G.:* Er——

*Announcer:* Use Omo for your underslip.
I give you Mary Smith of Cheam.

*F. G.:* Er——

*Announcer:* Use Omo and your smalls will gleam.
To keep your pillow shining white,
Lie on the bedroom floor all night.
In dancing you'll be a success
If you use Omo on your dress.

*F. G.:* If you're pushed for time to dry it,
Just dip it in deep fat and fry it.

*Announcer:* Or for the new burnt look we shove 'em
In a white hot kitchen oven.
O ma! O me! O my! O mo!
Now it's really time to go.

*Narrator:* She hastily pulls out the tub,
And frantically begins to scrub
Her old bedraggled grimy dress;
And—in a trice—you'd never guess
In spite of the rags she once had on
Looks as neat as the belle of Burlington.
Off with her slippers, on with her shoes,
Some eyeshadow out of the kitchen flues,
And her lips painted red with raspberry jam,

Making

<pre>                     She's really good; she aint no ham.
                     So she gives a twirl to her sister's brolly,
                     Helps herself to some housekeeping lolly,
                     And slithers out in the big black alley.
                     Cinders is bound for the Ball at the Palais!
                     So to the Palais, let us follow,
                     And see her beat her sisters hollow.
1st American:   Say, Willy, cop dat dame dere!
                     Boy, she's for me. She aint no square.
2nd American:  Leave off, Jake. She's far too sleek.
                     I like 'em nice and soft and weak.
Cinders:       Had your eyeful yet, you two?
2nd American:  You bet we have, and are we blue!
1st American:   Aw, quit the hokey-pokey, Bill.
                     Let's go look for jiving Jill.
Cinders:       I'll get Bert Nidget onto you.
Americans:     Nidget, Nidget! Boo hoo hoo!
Manager:       O.K. boys, if you want a brawl
                     Go down the Salvation Army Hall.
Bert:          Honey, you look swell tonight,
                     Dressed in that frock all gleaming white.
Cinders:       Yes, Omo did the trick for me.
                     It washes whiter than white can be.
Bert:          But where's the necklace you had on—
                     That real romantic pearly one?
Cinders:       O, that old string of plastic peas!
Bert:          Yes, the one you nicked from Selfridges.
Cinders:       Probably dropped it—must have done!
                     Oh, well—just have to nick another one!
Announcer:     One Two Three Four
                     Do you want to rock?
Cockey:                       No, cock.
Announcer:     Then bring your baby onto the floor.
Cinders:       Come on, Bert, let's dig this one.</pre>

93

## In Particular

| | |
|---|---|
| *Bert:* | O.K., ducks: we'll have some fun. |
| *Announcer:* | Rock your baby to and fro, |
| | Swing her round and away we go. |
| *Bert:* | Slow, slow, quick, quick, slow. |
| *Announcer:* | This isn't the Vic Sylvester show; |
| | So sling your babe and drag her back. |
| | Let's see her wobble inside that sack! |
| *Cinders:* | O Bert; just look at those other girls, |
| | All with their diamonds on and pearls. |
| *Bert:* | Diamonds like rocks and rubies like wedges. |
| *Cinders:* | My skirt is curling at the edges. |
| | I knew that I was wrong to fake it. |
| | I'll go to the Ladies' Room and shake it. |
| | O dear, Bert, I'll have to fly. |
| | Before the hem has shrunk too high. |
| *1st American:* | Say, brother, look: That dame looks flighty, |
| | Jiving there in her shorty nighty. |
| *Cinders:* | Omo's magic power's waning. |
| | I'll bash that Mrs. Bradshaw's brain in. |
| *2nd American:* | Say, Jake: that dame's gone running through. |
| | I vote we follow, me and you. |
| *Bert:* | Hey! Wait a minute. Here's your beads |
| | Stuck in the turn-up of my tweeds. |
| *1st American:* | Say, brother: where does she live, that blinder? |
| *Bert (coldly):* | I've no idea. |
| *2nd American:* | We'll help you find her. |
| *Bert:* | If you ask me, your offer's piffle. |
| *2nd American:* | We'll use the magic powers of skiffle. |
| *1st American:* | Yes, brother. We can give a hand |
| | To form a three piece skiffle band. |
| *2nd American:* | Sure, brother, we can find her place |
| | With Joe's guitar and my string base. |
| *1st American:* | So if you want to find your pretty, |
| | Just you compose a suitable ditty! |

# Making

| | |
|---|---|
| *Bert:* | I'll do anything to find my Cinders,<br>Shin up drains and climb in win*ders*. |
| *Announcer:* | That'll be all now; that'll be all.<br>This isn't the Brownie's charity ball.<br>You three suckers, quit your jive.<br>The cops are coming to close this dive. |
| *Bert:* | I know; I know; I know; I know:<br>I'll trace her little footsteps in the snow. |
| *2nd American:* | Oh brother! That's the very number.<br>Where'er she is she will not slumber. |
| *Narrator:* | And now in our delightful farce<br>The scene to Cinder's digs does pass. |
| *Cinders:* | I'll never see my Bert again;<br>All hopes of marriage down the drain,<br>Condemned to work my bones to blisters<br>Sweating for my ugly sisters.<br>Now let me scrub this beastly floor.<br>O, hark! I hear them at the door. |
| *1st Sister:* | O Cinders, what a ball you've missed.<br>Come here: I'll give your ear a twist. |
| *2nd Sister:* | We're off to bed, but don't you shirk.<br>Keep on scrubbing. Work and work! |
| *1st Sister:* | And after that, as soon as wink,<br>You'll tidy up the kitchen sink.<br>So get it polished up this minute,<br>You know I eat my porridge in it. |
| *Cinders:* | O go to bed, you silly old hag.<br>Don't stop here to rant and nag. |
| *Narrator:* | Off to bed go the ugly sisters;<br>Cinders sits and pops her blisters:<br>Snap, crackle, pop! they go,<br>And Cinders says: |
| *Cinders:* | O, O, O, O!<br>O what is that dull sound I hear |

Getting clearer and more near?
*The Skiffle Group sings, to the tune of 'Frankie and Johnnie':*
    Bertie went out with Cinders,
        And Cinders went out with Bert;
    Bertie was all over Cinders,
        And Cinders was all over dirt.

He was her man; but he done her in.

    Bertie took out his flick-knife,
        Cinders took off her shoe,
    Said 'Call me a heel once more, dear,
        And I'll beat the soul outa you!'

He was her man; but he done her in.

    Blood was all over the ceiling,
        Blood was all over the floor,
    Blood was the pattern on the carpets,
        Blood was running out of the door.

He was her man; but he done her in.

    Then Cinder's soul said to Bertie:
*Cinders:*      Don't stand out in the rain.
*Skiffle:*       If you speak to me like that, dear,
        I'll kill you all over again.

He was her man
*Cinders:*             So I'll let you in.
*Bertie:*       Cinders.
*Cinders:*      Bertie.
*Cinders (again):* Bertie!
*Bertie:*             Cinders!
    I've crawled down drains; I've climbed in
        win*ders.*
*Announcer:*   Someone's mother doesn't know

What someone's mother ought to know:  
What someone's mother ought to know  
In 'Omo washes whiter'.

*Bert:*       O Cinders, Cinders, Cinders, Cinders.  
*Cinders:*  O Bertie, Bertie, Bertie, Bertie:  
             Your hair awry; your shirt so dirty.  
*Bert:*       I sought you here; I sought you there.  
             I even went to Leicester Square.  
             I sang sweet songs in Piccadilly,  
             And drove the population silly.  
             O Cinders, what I want to know  
             Is where on earth we two can go.  
*Cinders:*  Cut the Hokey-Pokey, brother:  
             You'll have to come and live with mother.  
*Bert:*       O love is fine; but love is hard, O  
             You're as swell as Bridget Bardot.  
             Just one thing I want to know:  
             Does your mother use Omo?  
*Cinders:*  Of course she does. That's how I came  
             To be your pretty little flame.  
*Announcer:*  And whether you've enjoyed this,  
             Or whether it's made you sick,  
             It proves that Omo gets whites whiter  
             And gets whites whiter quick.

The tape-recorder can always be employed successfully with older age-groups for the sort of *bouts-rimés* compositions under consideration. Indeed, at this age, if operators with a fair knowledge of its techniques use the full lateral and direct qualities of sound to create depth and distance (as the B.B.C. does) and if one assembles the wherewithal to produce good sound effects, much can be achieved; and the play-back is even more rewarding than the composition.

The machine should only be run as a member of the group

indicates he has a line, and then switched off again. In the case of a play, it is a good idea to appoint each member as a different character. This more oral technique appeals in particular to older pupils; but there is no reason why it should not be used with young classes, except that they are generally greater in number and correspondingly more difficult to occupy near the recorder.

*Bouts-rimés* themselves are rewarding, especially if they try to produce humorous character sketches of every one in the form. Limericks and *bouts-rimés* limericks go well also.

Really good forms will be able to parody poetry they have read. I believe the parodying of compulsorily read poetry, e.g. G.C.E. exam poetry, to be a useful exercise as well as a useful therapy. It gives the pupils fresh insights, and it also helps them eliminate some of the frustrations occasioned by compulsory literature:

> It is an ancient schoolmaster
> And he sticketh one of three,
> By thy grey tweed and pimply tie,
> Now wherefore stick thou me?

There is no harm in this, a voluntary offering, and a fair ration of pleasure. After I was presented with it I set about writing some of my own. Parody, alas, eludes me. But I showed willing in their midst, and they took pleasure in my willingness and produced me enough further efforts to provide me with the wherewithal to enliven several lessons to other people.

If one is going to quote schoolboy to schoolboy, this is the most generous and innocuous way of doing it. Schoolboys may laugh at schoolboy howlers, but they become tense inside, and every time you invite them to mock at one of their fellows they become a little less sure of themselves. Parody for them, however, is a useful register of inadequacy. One teaches from it without teaching it away. To find how hard it is to be Coleridge, and yet to have the pleasure of mocking him, is a worthwhile education. And the laughter can be directed at the mockery, however gauche, and not the failure.

One often meets English teachers who maintain a vast store of triumphantly hoarded 'howlers'. These are the trophies natural to the subject, and they probably do no harm if the teacher does not become howler-minded. If his marking pencil is poised in anticipation of this rather mean delight he is not likely to regard his pupils' work with very much sympathy; and if he takes howlers back into the classroom to exhibit them for laughter he is doing positive harm. Progress in written work depends upon maintaining the natural growth of a relaxed and unconscious style. Normal correction is a great enough inhibition, without adding derision.

The classroom is not a lecture room; still less is it a courtroom. At most it is a workshop, with the teacher the master craftsman.

# 5. METHOD

THE TRANSITION between creative and 'received' work is an easy one, and any teacher sensitive enough to obtain good creative work from a class will not need me to tell him how to follow it up. Indeed, the direct consolidation of this sort of work depends so much upon the class that I doubt very much whether any general principles can be laid down, other than those implicit in the last chapter.

The only danger when the teacher attempts to equate creating with receiving is that a true balance seems impossible. What is received frequently overweighs the desire to create, and as this happens, the will to receive becomes rapidly exhausted as well.

What is the answer to this problem? There is no magic formula that can be devised to fit the interplay of teacher, subject, and class, and only a fool would suggest otherwise. Yet what cannot be averted can, in this case, easily be cured. A return to some more creative activity is indicated, for it is from the energies liberated by creation that the class derives the will to receive. If you do not agree with me about the part to be played by such activities, at least employ your own panacea: be it play-reading, an account of your last big-game hunt, or what you will; but do not continue to batter the poem against a hardening wall of resistance.

This is not method; it is common sense. But it has its corollary. Why invite such a situation in the first place? We all tend to do far too much received work in poetry. Very few short poems are worth spending much time on in class (by 'worth' I invoke an enjoyment quotient, of course), and the 'poetry programme' method, with sixteen assorted and selected, also has its limitations.

Far better is it to introduce a poem casually at the start of a period as one you've just enjoyed; or as one that seemed nearly as good as Jones R's poem about the bats (or whatever more elaborate confection you can muster); and then pass quietly on to something else. The impact will have been made; and this casual approach implies that looking for poems is a genial activity, with the result that members of class will be 'finding' poems before long, and reading them, too.

Or why not be a complete Charlatan? If you are up against any strict syllabus system, and few of us are lucky enough or conscienceless enough not to be, why not suddenly knock off ten minutes before the end of the worst lesson you can find in the week (Clause Analysis or Rules of Punctuation 4) and read a poem? By then even flagellation should be welcome, and boredom must not be underestimated as a teaching aid. If by any chance you have eliminated such ghastly manifestations from your syllabus, save a comic poem for the lesson that goes wrong because you just cannot make them see the point or because the caretaker has just been in to interrupt the lesson, and his observations do not sort well with *The Shepherd's Life*.

The danger to much of our teaching is the intractability of the forty-minute period as a unit of effort. Too often we design our work with this purely artificial factor in mind; and for the arts, especially the intense arts like poetry, such a length of time can be fatal. Besides, poetry in the classroom so often depends upon opportunism that it is impossible always to anticipate it and prepare for it. For this reason one should never commit oneself absolutely to teaching any one thing in any given period.

What of lesson preparation? This should not be disregarded,

surely? Of course not; but ideally, in English teaching, one should consider a larger unit of time. One could plan a week's work fairly thoroughly, for example, but much of its ordering, when planned, should be left to chance.

This all seems obvious enough; but once more an excellent and accepted general principle is frequently overlooked in the teaching of poetry. It is often felt to be difficult; therefore it is afforded its sullen last period on Wednesday afternoon when both teacher and class know what to expect and can play safely for time together. I said earlier that no-poetry is better than poetry-without-pleasure. Think how easy it is to turn for a mere five minutes to Ogden Nash or some other 'Comic and Curious Verse'. Is there really any teenage form that would fail to appreciate

> A window-cleaner in our street
> Who fell (five storeys) at my feet
> Impaled himself on my umbrella.
> I said: 'Come, come, you careless fella!
> If my umbrella had been shut
> You might have landed on my nut.'

And if they once come to expect poetry to be enjoyed the battle is won. I am not worried by the fact that such poetry is not 'great'. It at least has the unassailable educational dignity of humour, and this is more than can be said for the majority of slushy rhymes that find their way into school anthologies. These wretched books are the greater part of one's trouble. But I anticipate.

All I propose to do at the moment is reiterate two simple points. The first is that poetry must not be isolated, critically or creatively, from the remainder of one's syllabus. The second is that it must not be overweighted. If it is seen always in relation to the class enjoyment of it, it is not likely to be.

Successful poetry teaching depends upon a number of other mainly psychological factors which are also controlled by the English teacher. Although any sense of 'work' should be avoided, there is no reason why the sense of mystery should not be enlarged, in particular that good down-to-earth idea of mystery that was cognate with 'mastery' in Medieval England.

Books as books are objects to be revered. This is not a subject for repeated exhortation; nothing is more frustrating for a pupil than to be given a battered and tattered piece of literature and ordered to treat it gently. Books only come to be revered as objects, to develop associations of mystery, when they are explained as objects. A number of lessons on book-production, with prepared examples, are intensely valuable in this respect, and they are direct and factual enough (if well illustrated and demonstrated) to command complete class interest. The history of printing, printing itself, with some consideration of type-faces, methods of folding and cutting, paper-production, and binding—these are all useful lessons. Pupils should be encouraged to bring old copies, for class comment. Indeed, there is no reason why a fairly good display should not be built up in school. A new book should be classified sometimes when it is given out; the pupils encouraged to discover, by noting the sheet letters, whether it is bound quarto, octavo, and so on. When such a system is in operation, poetry benefits immensely. Poetry books should be among the most excitingly produced books, because of the opportunities they offer for good typography. If they are not excitingly produced, there is not very much point in ordering them for school. The topic may sound dull: but its factual nature always makes it successful.

Speech, dramatic ability, and lack of self-consciousness on the part of one's pupils, have a great bearing on the successful teaching of poetry. Good speech, in this context, does not necessarily mean a mastery of English syntax and pronunciation. This would certainly be asking the impossible and, to many regional teachers, the undesirable. It means that the pupil should have been encouraged to discover the dramatic and tonal qualities of his own voice. If he has been taught according to the methods suggested in the chapter on making poetry, or if choral speech is pursued as a creative rather than as a received activity, he will already have made this discovery, and he will be a good instrument for verse reading. The pupil's voice obviously constitutes one of the most important media for the enjoyment of a poem, as well as of other literature. No amount of education in 'received speech' will help poetry lessons, however. The pupil has to realize that his voice is a versatile rather than a flawless instrument. He will learn more from one programme of the Goon Show than from a year's course with a speech therapist.

There is one other general point to consider; that is the matter of frankness, frankness in expressing opinions, frankness in dealing with material. One cannot have frankness in a lesson if the class feels that there are taboo subjects; yet some taboos there must be.

There should certainly not be any artistic taboos: Dan Dare, Prudence Kitten, and the junior comics that use rhyme, are all part of the English scene; that much is already clear. But one's very approach to these matters often invokes professional taboos: 'Please, sir, Mr. Crabb thinks Dan Dare is a complete waste of time.' Such a challenge can be most unpleasant if one has established that the *Eagle Comic* is the child's only reading, and consequently decided that this slender but bright flame needs all the fanning one can give it; but it is not an excuse for polemics against the more conservative wisdom of Mr. Crabb. One should long ago have established the fact that good taste is a matter of opinion. English is not a cranky subject, and whatever the provocation one should always work for professional unity, on educational as much as professional grounds. The child needs, morally, a sense of communal rectitude in its teaching staff; artistically it requires to be assured of a pervading atmosphere of tolerance.

The last, and most difficult taboo, relates to sex. One cannot make any clear distinction between 'adult' and 'non-adult' literature on purely artistic grounds, so it is most unwise to add censorship to the general problem of selection of material. At some stage, more mature classes have to read literature that deals with the relationship between man and woman: it is important to make it clear that literature describing this relationship is as wholesome a part of human experience as the relationship itself. It would be stupid on more general grounds to intrude coarse-grained literature into the form-room; and the 'love story' itself, whether frankly or ambiguously portrayed, is rarely suitable material; but it is wrong to treat sixth-form Chaucer in too hermetic a manner. The Miller is just as important as the Knight in the Chaucerian canon, and he is far more useful as propaganda.

For teenagers, sex becomes an immediate problem; it is their first real contact with adult maturity. Literature that touches upon its relationships had best be in the modern idiom, lest their sense of its archaism leads them to reject it; and since love-poetry is nearly always 'off centre' in idiom it had better not be read at all—devotional love poetry, that is. There is nothing wrong with *Frankie and Johnnie*; but the average class in its early and middle teens does not respond too happily to Keats's 'Pillowed upon my fair love's ripening breast. To hear for ever its soft fall and swell;' and the word 'swoon' which comes in the last couplet is particularly unfortunate. One's Teddy Boys masticate with empty jaws in wide-eyed silence.

So much for general practice. What of particular lessons?

## In Particular

As the two previous chapters have stressed, age is the most important governing factor. Although it is impossible to look for any standard eleven-year-old response one *can* expect a standard type of development; and when a class is, collectively, at a certain stage it is wise to be on the watch for symptoms of a change in taste or for any signs that the class is becoming impatient of a certain technique.

Impatience, by the by, is not symptomatized by unrest. I am not talking about indiscipline. There is a type of teacher who regards it as 'soft' to take his cues from his class; but the good teacher recognizes dissatisfaction in his class before the class recognizes it in itself. It is when the transference of interest becomes first conscious and then deliberate that the real damage is done. Such a loss of interest is generally the result of accumulated bad·teaching. For a moment let us consider one or two examples of this:

There is a very common type of unsuccessful lesson. We can call it 'The-culture-in-strange-places or the-poet-is-just-an-ordinary-sort-of-bloke' approach. It goes like this:

*Teacher:* Not all poets are soft, you know. Take for example Wolfe Uppingham. Uppingham was a young subaltern in the Tank Corps. I say 'was' because he died playing a very gallant part in a most decisive action.

> (By now a boy's class will be interested in spite of itself, and the master now digresses, amid respectful silence on what hell it was in the Desert, till we get:)

He used to write poetry out there, you know; sitting by his tank, under the stars. There's a piece called 'Sunset Stand-to'. It goes like this:

> O pimply night, O putrefying moon,
> O palpitating warble of the loon,

> O light, alight! Alight, O love
> And little fishes and the stars above
>
> O Lord. . . .

Once more a good biographical story has been let down by a bad or unsuitable poem.

Equally unsuccessful is the following approach, which we can call 'The double-take method':

> I've got a rather exciting description here. It's of a bullfight. I found it in an old newspaper cutting and I thought it would interest you.
>
> (Reads long, exciting, and lurid account.)
>
> That was an enjoyable way to talk about it, wasn't it? But it's not the only way, you know. Listen to this, for example:
>
> (Reads poem by Roy Campbell, George Barker, or some such. . . .)

The poem's chance has been completely spoiled because it has been unfavourably compared with a realistic piece of prose. Such an approach shows that the teacher thoroughly misunderstands the nature of the poem, in any event.

There is a similar related mistake, 'The Poetry-in-Your-Life' method:

> That was a very good half-century Barton made for the school yesterday, wasn't it? Well-played, Barton! I wonder if you chaps know Francis Thompson's poem about cricket. . . .

All of these methods have one psychological fault in common. They evoke strong expectations and then fail to satisfy them.

Even well-chosen poems would have failed, because they would not have been allowed to stand alone.

There is one more point: each of these introductions uses the would-be sleight-of-hand approach that is so widely extolled by educational theorists. In reality, it is quite impossible to transfer interest, or at least in the wrong direction. Keith Douglas's poem on the '88 Gunner' is a good one and it goes down well in class; his prose description in *From Alemein To Zem Zem* of a tank battle is also good, and it too goes down well. I take care my classes hear the poem first. The tank-battle enriches the poem. The class does not have its wide conceptions of 'tank-battle', 'desert', etc., suddenly limited by the cold word 'poem'.

In the next chapter I mention many methods of presenting poetry. These are so numerous that one could set down specimen lessons *ad lib* and probably *ad nauseam*; and it is to avoid doing this that I have mapped out the boundaries of less successful areas first. I also said that most poetry lessons were probably too long. Yet in the Junior School they can afford to be long; the interest is sufficient for them to expand and ripen. May I therefore record, as well as I am able, a lesson at which I was privileged to be present? It was taught by a pupil of mine to a mixed class, small town Stream B, age 7–8. It went like this:

*Teacher:* Well, I thought it would be great fun if we had a poem today. It's about a Knight—yes, I thought you would be interested—a very old pernickety Knight called Sir Nickety Nox. Shall I read it to you? Good. Here it goes, then:

> (He read the whole poem in a perfectly straightforward fashion—for the age group. That is, he overplayed the dramatic pause after the first line,

and he dwelt lovingly upon the poem's gnarled vocabulary and other triumphant peculiarities.)

That sounded good, didn't it? Wait a minute, I've got it written out on the other side of the board. Can everybody read it? Good. Now who's going to read it out for us all to hear? John is a good reader. While he's reading it we can all follow it. Right you are, John.

That was very good. Anybody else? Oh, everybody else. Well, I'll tell you what: David can read the first verse, Mary the second, and Andrew the third.

That sounded excellent. Let's do that one again with some different readers. Only this time we'll all say the name, 'Sir Nickety Nox' each time it occurs.

Very good. I think we know the poem now. We shall soon be able to have some fun with it. Let's say it all together. One, two, three.

Much too loud, but great fun. Let's hear the girls do it by themselves.

Now the boys, in a whisper.

I know. Suppose the boys all become Knights, and read the lines about the Knight, in a deep voice; and the girls become wives and daughters and read their lines. Is everybody sure about that? Good. Can I just say the title, please? I can?

And so it went on. It was successful because it had had simplicity and variety; and because the teacher was light and unobtrusive in manner, and merely encouraged the class to enjoy itself. Any tricks in such a lesson would have been a distraction; so would the use of more elaborate aids. And, of course, the *tour de force* teacher, the usual sort of grade A educational bogey, who hurls himself at a class with versatile energy and seeks to engulf it with the irresistible wave of his own enthusiasm, would have failed miserably. It is all too easy to over-teach poetry. There are some volatile liquids that effervesce rapidly when allowed to come in contact with the fresh air. One does not shake the bottle to achieve this effect. One merely lifts off the stopper.

This point, indeed the very lesson under consideration, brings us to the whole problem of class enthusiasm. At one stage the young teacher found his charges were becoming too rowdy; but it was the type of rowdyism that showed that his lesson was going well rather than otherwise. To dampen such enthusiasm would be both to bewilder the class and to ruin the lesson. I thought he applied the brake in a most unobtrusive fashion.

Yet it is precisely this that many teachers are unable to do. The tentative, shy person who is very much alive to class reaction is often the person who finds something that started well has flared up out of control, and who sets about drowning it in hysteria, however adult its form. Forewarned should be forearmed. One can expect such problems if one does the job well; and as I said earlier it is this sort of teacher who, realizing his or her limitations, will in the long run do the job best. The robust personality, handling the mood of his class just as a child handles plasticine, is not likely to succeed with poetry; he will fail at the end of his introduction. The good teacher is the person who can invoke a creative mood in a few well-chosen words, and then stand aside while the class works at its enjoyment. His lessons are a matter of quiet strategy rather than flamboyant tactics. That does not prevent him from being an opportunist, however.

So much for the poetry lesson at the Primary School, which is, after all, predominantly the place for the 'poetry lesson', as distinct from the shorter time units indicated earlier in the chapter. Such a simple and repetitive method cannot be employed again until pupils are much older, until one is prepared to employ many more aids. I have spent long periods of time on single poems with teenagers and with adults; but in the context of choral speech, and here it should be realized that the poem is not seen by most of a group as possessing any intrinsic merit. It is seen rather as a blue print for something else. However, this problem is dealt with in a separate chapter.

With the next age-group, approximately the '11 plus', techniques should be predominantly creative. This is easily the most profitable period for creative work, and for creative introductions to received work. But I should also expect a large number of 'short lessons' to be inserted into other periods, as well as a somewhat smaller number of 'long lessons', presented according to the methods listed in the next chapter. For example, once a term I should expect a class symposium of poems gleaned from anthologies, another symposium of home reading, and at least one of members' own contributions. I should encourage these to be accompanied by discussion.

If these go well I include my own symposium, making use of rehearsed readers. Sometimes, with Machiavellian intention, but complete cultural honesty, I do a symposium of poems I do not like in a given anthology. This generally increases quite substantially the number of poems the class likes. Sometimes again I allow them to do their own 'don't like' symposiums, as the finest sort of prelude to healthy artistic war.

All of these 'lessons' mean one thing: I am heard very little and they—and their poems—are heard a very great deal. I do not figure as the sponsor of anything other than free speech and enjoyment; and this is quite the safest cultural sponsorship.

This may seem cowardly; it appears to represent very little activity. Does it, in fact? In a twelve-week term, quite apart from frequent creative activity, there would be about four full 'received lessons', plus a considerable number (at least one a week) of the 'short lessons'. This is far better than the regular dull Wednesday afternoon: the subject stays fresh and unpredictable; it is presented in a creative context in that members find their own poems; and because they find their own poems they have to undergo the weighty educational process —quite uncatered for by the Wednesday afternoon-style—of looking for them.

This does not mean that poems should never be talked about. Certain poems can stand being talked about an awful lot, even with thirteen-year-olds. But what those poems are and what one should find to say about them I have thought fit to deal with in the chapter on Material.

It is the next age—14–15—that is the really difficult one, so difficult that I would leave it to Comic Poetry and another chapter if my conscience would let me. After all, it is largely choice of material that is involved. However, there are some escape clauses.

As a general principle: I should expect to take any class I had taught for the previous two years through this period without much difficulty. Initially there would be a fair amount of impetus to aid one; then as it slackened I should concentrate on a very few Comic or vigorous symposium lessons, and some comic creative verse sketches of the sort noticed earlier; while individual lessons would make the maximum use of aids, particularly the right sort of gramophone records and the prepared record. If I am asked to take over such a class for the first time I am profoundly unhappy; and modern school and grammar school teachers will know why.

We will suppose the worst, however—we either do not already know the class or, because of waning enthusiasm, are unable to exploit our knowledge by means of inherited techniques. What do we do? Like Capek's snails we 'lie low' until we have succeeded in moving the class our way a little. We then, piecemeal, disseminate humorous literature. 'Poetry' is not mentioned. Short passages of prose, jokes even, providing they turn upon a nice witticism, and very short comic verses, each only four to eight lines long, become the contents of frequent but brief offerings at the start of lessons, generally casually introduced as if they are something discovered in general reading the previous evening.

The material for these interludes is easy to find. To avoid sending the reader to another chapter, one should mention, for prose camouflage, back numbers of *Argosy*, *Reader's Digest*, Daily Telegraph's '*Way of the World*' (a collection has been published), '*Beachcomber*', any old *Timothy Shy's*, The New Statesman's '*This England*', *Punch*, of course, newspapers in general; for verse, The New Statesman and Spectator competitions (when really topical, i.e. the ones on Teddy Boys and Rock and Roll), *The Penguin Book of Comic and Curious Verse* and its sequel, any newspaper competition collection of limericks, and back numbers of almost anything like the old *Lilliput*. Even the old *Chums Annual* has afforded some excellent limericks. This is only scratching the surface; but it represents a start. The two Penguin books by themselves offer an abundance of scope.

In brief, one needs to avoid treating verse as significant literature, and instead, concentrate on it as humorous expression. One should not aim at establishing any sort of ascendancy over other forms of expression. One wants merely to keep it in the ring.

With a responsive class far more can be achieved. There is one profitable area of literary experience to be explored at this age: that is violence. The poetry of violence is difficult to find, and the mood is hard to sustain. For that reason I deal rather fully with sources in the chapter on Material.

Fortunately, in the modern school and in the more difficult

classes of the grammar school, one is provided with an ideal introduction and source in skiffle music and the American folk ballad. In a year or two, tastes may alter; though the cowboy with his guitar has been a reasonably acceptable symbol for many years. In that case, the teacher will have to turn to 'Pop' music, repugnant though the term is. He will have to turn somewhere.

If one's interest in these subjects—and it need only be interest not approval—appears to be genuine then one can obtain very real results. With pupils interested in skiffle I have had long and interesting discussions on the lyrics and ballads in the Alan Lomax collection. I have had similar worthwhile contacts when talking about 'the Blues'. After school we sometimes listen to one another's records. More important, we look at books. Your skiffle player in particular is generally quite a bookish person, with at least the Pan collection of ballads somewhere about him.

What do such activities achieve? They create an atmosphere of interest and energy. Generally poetry itself becomes a part of this atmosphere; quite certainly it can never hope to exist otherwise.

This brings us to a most vital point. The policy of artistic and creative integration mentioned in the opening chapters yields very great rewards with this difficult age group. It is generally accepted that an English teacher should be a person of wide interests. He had better take good care that his interests are as wide as his pupils'.

If he can present his class with a wide cultural front, if television, cinema, jazz, advertising-jingles, and comic papers are as much a part of his make-up as Shakespearean soliloquies, then at least he will cultivate reciprocal interests in his class. Give-and-take is the basis of educational exchange. I founded a Jazz Club at school once; its members were exactly the people I expected to find there—the fact that many of them belonged to nothing else was to my mind a very good justification for the existence of just such a club. A term later I founded a poetry-reading circle. When I attended the first reading I found there all the members of the Jazz Club.

Most important, the more interests in common one has with one's pupils, the more genuine—as opposed to artificial —introductions can one make to one's subject. The early teenager is increasingly conscious of the differences that exist between himself and his teachers, in matters of taste, dress, habits of speech, and ambitions. It is no use saying to him, 'I like Beethoven'. His reaction is, 'You are the sort of person who likes Beethoven, and that's not my sort of person at all'. If one says, 'Do you like Burl Ives too? So do I. What do you think of Beethoven?' then at least one is not standing exactly on the opposite side of the fence. It also gives one an area for manœuvre. Likes in his territory allow one to have dislikes in his territory. One can like Burl Ives but dislike Lonnie Donegan, and he will appreciate this. And at once one has overcome the great bogey of teenage rebelliousness. He sees that one does not have to like everything, that one can pick and choose. He will probably concede you Donegan if you concede Beethoven. Next week he may be listening to Mozart. More than this: frown at his likes and one misses the chance of appealing to his inherent intellectual snobbery. Everybody is an intellectual snob: it is largely a matter of chance whether the taste is for Middle Scottish Poetry or weights for the two o'clock at Newmarket. If a teacher likes everything the pupil likes and then some more, a great responsibility is placed upon the pupil's ego. If the teacher does not like anything the pupil likes then the teacher has no place in the pupil's world. The pupil supposes there must be other people like his teacher, but not in *his* street, thank you.

You will see how inextricably this is all bound up with one's overall approach to material. To this subject I have thought it best to devote another chapter.

Lest such a sudden ending seems to avoid the problems involved in senior grammar school teaching and work elsewhere for related exams, I shall also deal with this topic separately in the chapter entitled 'Examining'.

# 6. MEANS

A VERY REAL problem in the teaching of poetry is to know how, physically, the poem can be presented to the class. It simply does not do to say, 'Take out your poetry books and turn to page thirty-four', if one knows that a battered, brown-looking book will be reluctantly fished out of desks, and that the poem on page thirty-four has already had its chances of success nullified by the patent dullness of the rest of the poems in the book. Yet in most schools that is likely to be the situation.

How should the teacher regard the poetry anthology? The best way to answer this is to ask how the class *does* regard the poetry anthology in question. If it is a clean, new book, with carefully chosen and well-presented material, obviously it has its uses, and one would be foolish to ignore them. But it should be realized as a good general principle that the actual content of the average anthology is dull and rarely has anything to recommend it. Even a good anthology generally has only a few poems *that will suit a given teacher who is dealing with a given class.* Even a very good anthology cannot eliminate these two intensely personal factors, and at best it can only be a suggestive variorum.

From this fact a number of practical considerations arise.

One could give out such an anthology and encourage the class to dip into it, select poems they themselves like, and then recommend that they are read together. One can even suggest that individuals pick out their own favourites and present them themselves.

*In Particular*

This is a very good system if one is not ambitious for the anthology (i.e. if one sees the problem in perspective). On two different occasions I have used this approach exclusively with classes. In each case the anthology was one very well known in teaching circles. In each case the class enjoyed about half a dozen poems between them, and agreed to enjoy three collectively. The exercise, the feeling of freedom to pick and choose, was a most valuable one, and it enabled a fair amount of pleasure to be obtained and several critical and expository skills to be exercised. But it also indicated the limitations of two well-known anthologies.

If one has a number of anthologies it pays to keep a central pool. Indeed, when buying poetry books one should never buy more than one class-size set of any one book. No book is worth—in terms of pleasure—leaving with a form for more than a term at the very outside. Ideally, if an issue system is preferred, a period of a few weeks should be regarded as the maximum.

A strong central pool should obviate the need to issue poetry, however. If one has half a dozen different anthologies, and each of these contains three poems which seem good to the individual teacher and seem to him likely to please the class, then one has a substantial number of poems that can be presented by means of the printed page. For the first six occasions on which the books are issued they will be new and unrecognized. Six is a large enough number also for the class to return quite freshly to the first book when the others have been used once before. So by issue and return of a number of different anthologies on a single lesson rota one can obtain very favourable associations of pleasure, or—at the least— prevent unpleasurable associations from recurring too frequently.

So much for the presentation by means of the printed page. It should not be assumed, of course, that a successful presentation means that all that is desirable has been accomplished, nor that a satisfactory solution will continue to be so if it is applied over and over again. I try to give my own classes an anthology to keep, if possible for a term, and issue sets of others for a period at a time. Towards the end of term, when a given set of books is not likely to be specifically required again for the class, I combine the advantages of both methods by allowing them to look through. If the book, pleasant in layout, has been associated with two good poems and two good lessons, it is surprising to see how eagerly the class seize the opportunity to explore it. They have never been *prevented* from so doing before, of course; it is merely that they have never had time to do so while dealing with single poems.

There are a number of other methods of presenting pupils with a text, but these are not always satisfactory. In theory, poems can be typed and stencilled, and so circulated on single pieces of paper. Such a method is often praised because it eliminates, so it is said, stale associations occasioned by a known text-book, and because it provides no distracting influences in the shape of pages that can be turned to reveal subjects other than the one in hand. The last argument is purely negative, of course, and insufficient to recommend any method of instruction; and my answer to the former is to invite its advocates to look at the faces of the class as they give out their bundles of paper. Even if the reproduction is smooth (and how infrequently it is for one reason or another), even if letters are unclogged and the work well set out, there is something so uncouth about a typewriter's method of leading and gapping that it repels most people almost instantly. If, for reasons sufficiently good or in circumstances sufficiently bad, one feels compelled to use this method then use the Banda system, which sets limpid and coloured type on a glossy paper. The result is far more pleasant to read and handle. If the school does not own such a machine, and one has to use one of the porous-paper methods, I would like to recommend (as do their makers but not most educational supply offices) that the stencil is printed off on a coloured porous paper. These can be obtained in pink, green, blue, and yellow, and the coloured background is far more attractive.

For younger children one can also reproduce free-hand illustrations by means of the Banda and these greatly reinforce the text. The same thing can be achieved with some other methods.

Some English masters gain the co-operation of the Art Department and have beautifully illuminated texts prepared on cartridge paper in coloured indian inks. I have elsewhere hinted at the possibility of co-operation between these two departments: I hasten to say that this is not a suitable case. The scribes will come to hate the poem, whatever pleasure it may subsequently give to others, for lettering is a most distasteful process and quite certainly one that most sympathetic art masters will be unwilling to have their pupils undertake.

If there is a printing press in the school, and some schools are this fortunate, the case is far different, and full use should be made of the opportunity. After all, the setting up of poetry does bring out the most interesting lessons in typography, and it can be appreciated as such. But alas, only a few schools at present have any real facilities for printing. The more resource-ful teacher can always take an evening course in printing at his local technical school, of course, and put his practical work to good use. It may even be possible to suborn the entire printing department, for 'prentice printers are always happy to do useful work.

Some teachers dismember old poetry books and mount in-dividual poems on strong coloured paper. This is initially a good idea, and it certainly makes a change, especially for a younger class. Unfortunately the resulting 'broadsheets' are not very durable and quickly become dog-eared. Since only very old stock can be subjected to the initial depredation involved, it is highly unlikely that the copy itself will be particularly sparkling, either.

In spite of the drawbacks involved in using this method to obtain complete sets of a single poem, it obviously has great advantages if one is content to create mixed sets. A book of suitable comic poems could be broken up and some twenty pieces mounted on cards. One could then use these on an exchange system, with the form passing the different poems around. This would result in a very interesting period. It is certainly a method worth trying, and, since it involves the sacrifice of only one book, far more up-to-date material and a cleaner page can be obtained for it. The reader may wonder at my insistence on the comic poem. Quite apart from its application in class, there is one intensely practical reason. That is that the comic collection does have a unifying theme. Even a dunce, setting out to pick out *all* comic poems, will pick *some* comic poems. Hence the comic anthology is one best converted.

A placard or roller with a poem printed on it in large type, generally needing to be hand-blocked by the teacher, can be employed to advantage with younger children; but it is not a method to overdo. A young class can be made to enthuse about anything, but there is something strangely repellent about too much black ink on calico, and except for variety there is nothing to recommend this method above the use of the blackboard. Coloured chalk and a good board technique are never to be belittled, especially with young classes.

As a last really workable method of visual presentation the pupil's own 'Poetry Book' is an entirely sound idea. In it he keeps not only his own poems but any other poems he likes enough to copy out. If he is given a free hand he generally likes anything, by the time he has finished copying it, however haphazardly or desperately his mind has first seized upon it. Conversely he would dislike even what he would normally enjoy, if compelled to copy that one poem without any choice.

One is always coming up against this basic education truth: an artificial choice must be presented even when no absolute choice exists. An 'either-or' choice is generally as satisfying to the pupil as a 'yes-no' choice; and although one must never be frightened of offering the latter choice in poetry, one is a fool to present it too often. Good education gives the pupil a choice of activities, not a choice between activity and inertia. The poetry book seems to me very good education indeed. One should never insist that the book be kept very neatly. It is a copy-book, and given a fair chance and some incentive most children are neat. Too many teachers overlook the fact that a person is generally as neat as he or she can be.

I have spent a long time dealing with the practical aspects of visual presentation. There are many less practical ones, of course. There is a very good 'John Gilpin' filmstrip, for example, and—if one can pretend it is part of something else —one can often slip into other contexts a verse or two on a home-made slide. It rather depends upon one's competence as a charlatan. It never does to be caught by one's class practising the type of casual deception that one's educational tutors so frequently extol. It would, if one were energetic, be possible to combine, with episcope and diascope, some Coghill translation of the *Canterbury Tales* with the excellent filmstrip that exists on the characters, for example. Or one might spend thirty colour exposures on rhyming tombstones, market-crosses and the like. Or one might not.

Indeed, one should ask oneself whether the class is not by now a little tired of looking at poems. The single sense grows weary, and the eye longs to sleep in the ear. Just as one exercises different senses at different times in the lesson, so one should not rely exclusively on any one for the preliminary presentation of material.

The human voice and poetry go well together, and nearly all the poems that pass my test in the next chapter as being suitable for class will be found to emerge coherently when listened to. The basic quality of immediate coherence must always be sought for classroom poetry.

Elsewhere I shall talk about oral class participation in the development of a poem. These few simple precepts only take one as far as presenting it.

One can always use one's own voice, reading or reciting. One can even ask the class to listen to it on a tape-recorder. This last idea is not merely an attempt to present the ordinary, once removed. One can seek a rehearsed perfection with the recorder; for a young—or an uninhibited class—one can also produce background effects if necessary, and very enlivening they can be. A dialogue between oneself and recorder is also easy to obtain. Such poems as Kipling's 'Danny Deever' or Auden's 'O what is that sound?' lend themselves to this sort of treatment. One records one's more recondite bath-tap or shaving-mirror voice for parts like the colour-sergeant, and dialogues-in-class with one's normal voice. Members of class can also take turns to recite question and answer in conjunction with one's ghostly half. Great fun they will find it, too. Enough amusing bad timings will occur to make things really enjoyable. A big mistake when using aids is to equate them always with perfection. One is not a conjuror; and by aiming at a self-consciously flawless performance with aids one can all too easily encourage a brittle atmosphere. Reasonable preparation eliminates reasonable error. The crux of good teaching is not to worry about what difficulties are likely to arise but examine what constructive use can be made of them.

One should not forget the three-dozen voices at one's disposal—the voices belonging to the class. A very good approach is to start the lesson by handing a pupil a copy of a poem, printed or otherwise, and tell him that you will require his assistance shortly, requesting him meanwhile to look through the piece he is to read. This is a particularly good method with a less eager class; and the best person to ask to read is the most recalcitrant pupil. I do not know why it is, but by some psychological freak a pupil always takes a kindly interest in something he has to help present, no matter how foreign it is to his nature; and by the same token the class will always accept anything passed on to them by the form nuisance. The idea that a member of the class is ahead of them also puts the rest on their mettle.

This method is even better employed when one wishes to have a number of poems read. The books can be dotted round the class, and one can introduce the poems how one will, or even have them read in a preselected order. In the previous chapter there are some derogatory remarks about certain types of introductions to poems. Strangely enough, when one is introducing work that will be read by class members one can succeed with almost any introduction. Even those castigated elsewhere become nearly acceptable. For maximum effect, one wishes to hand out contemporary collections of work: the bright covers and flaring print of modern book jackets should be exploited to the full. The idea that poetry comes out of dull-looking books should be vigorously dispelled.

Using these methods one should alternate the possibilities of formal declaration from the front of the form with a more casual recital from the pupil's normal position in the classroom. One should always seek to employ imported talent as well. If one has a rehearsed choral-speaking group in a certain class, its aid should be enlisted for performance in front of other classes. This is valuable from several points of view. It persuades the recipients that they are not the only people who 'do' poetry in the school; and it generally confronts them with a standard of competence higher than they fancy themselves capable of achieving, for school children grow so used to their own talent that they never cease to marvel at outsiders of similar ability. It is also good for the performers, as it stimulates their sense of self-importance and gives them a platform upon which to display it. Indeed, the senior recalcitrant of one class, after his sterling performance to his own confrères, is a promising candidate for praise; and he can generally be persuaded to learn and rehearse his wares for export. In fairness to him, he should always be exhibited in conjunction with other artists. One must combat any idea that a child is becoming a sort of solo freak, even if he enjoys freaking before strange faces—and he rarely does.

Earlier I said that one should not expect perfection in a poetry lesson. Part of one's trouble arises from such a mistaken expectation. In a normal lesson a teacher looks for occasional roughnesses. He is not worried by the fact that Jones minor fluffs an occasional line, or that Smith pronounces 'misled' as 'mizzled', in a normal play-reading period. Obviously if one places a poetry lesson at the mercy of the Smiths and Joneses of a class one can expect the same mistakes in like measure. If the teacher has cultivated the usual relaxed atmosphere, such mistakes are no more damaging in one lesson that in another. The danger, however, is that the teacher is all too often on the defensive when dealing with poetry. The tight-lipped 'don't-you-dare-try-anything-on' look is hardly suitable; and it does no good to rebuke a genuinely accidental error. A laughing 'Hard luck! I think we had better take that one again' very quickly restores the poise of a lesson; there is no need for poetry to be immediately brittle. The person who thinks it is a sacred activity had better not take it into the classroom.

Far more reliable voices are to be found upon gramophone records, however; and a sensible use of recorded poetry can bring real pleasure to classes. Bernard Miles reading 'Danny Deever', John Laurie reading border ballads—the very fibre of such voices gives a tremendous masculine authority to the spoken word.

There is very little to say about recorded poetry. It is never worth indulging in unless the school playing equipment is sound, of course. Otherwise there are few pitfalls. Most of the big recording companies advertise poetry discs in their normal lists, and nearly all local libraries keep a fair selection of speech records. Similarly the school-and-subject libraries should seek to build up a collection.

To facilitate this, the British Council publish yearly a complete list of all recorded poetry. Their address is:

Recorded Sound Department,
The British Council,
65 Davies Street,
London W.1.

There is also a poetry anthology, 'Poems to Read and Hear', which only includes recorded poetry, and which lists at the back the records concerned. It is quite pleasantly presented, and I would rate it as a 'six-poem' anthology (fairly high praise), so it is worth obtaining for its own sake.

There is one word of warning: poetry records vary enormously in quality; so one should be careful when buying for the class. There are too many thin-voiced women and high-voiced men on record. What is required is a poem that answers the general requirements of the class in itself, and that is given unity and distinction by a strong, slightly coarse-textured voice. Such records are rare.

I have purposely left B.B.C. school's broadcasts to the last. They are committed, for obvious reasons, to 'good' poetry, and this is rarely suitable for the classroom; and they are hampered by the lack of contact with their audience; and some sense of reciprocal participation is essential in the teaching of poetry, as I said earlier. They are further hampered by the wide age—and intelligence—groups they have to cater for. This means that there is only a slight chance that they will ever produce anything suitable for a given teacher and given class, even supposing one can achieve coincidence of time-table with the broadcast.

However, the situation can be improved on. It is possible that from time to time they will broadcast something that will seem possible for a given class. One does not wish, one dare not wish, ever to play a programme direct to a class, without first hearing it. B.B.C. readers are excellent; but the effect of some voices on some classes has to be seen to be believed. Therefore the programme should be taken off on to the tape-recorder and vetted. This means that one can introduce the programme as one wishes. It also means that, in the rare event of a broadcast being suitable, one has a record of a first-class reading for future use.

# 7. MATERIAL

EING ABLE to choose suitable poetry for the classroom is
an acquired art for most people. Given time, a fair
knowledge of the byways rather than the highways
of English poetry (though what university or training
college English course indicates the former; and how many
English teachers have a really competent knowledge of the
latter?)—given a willingness to sense the tastes of the class
from negative rather than positive evidence—most of us will
ultimately arrive at a fair degree of competence.

Time, alas, is our enemy. Each failure to find really suitable
material makes it more difficult to gain the willing attention
of the class next time. The older the pupil the less resilient
does he become to disappointment. The most elaborately
conceived introductions are wasted; and after a time one
senses that a class that will listen with real interest while one
introduces a topic will 'switch off' when the topic itself is
reached. Sometimes this is caused by one's inability to manage
the transition comfortably, but this is rare, for the transition
between oneself and the poem is a physical one, and the class
is accustomed to making it. More frequently any failure here
is a conditioned reflex. The pupil has been disappointed
before. Something has not lived up to the exaggerated claims
that have been made for it. Why should it this time? And we
cannot afford to sidle into a poetry lesson. We must open
with vigour and confidence—and it had better not be mis-
placed confidence. Granted that a good lesson is something
like a conjuring trick; it must be a real rabbit that comes out

of the hat. We all know the teacher or lecturer who rallies us breezily to enjoy a subtlety or to surmount an obstacle. We are carried along with him eagerly enough until we discover that there is no subtlety or no obstacle. As adults we cannot be fooled like this twice; a teenager can hardly be trifled with more often, nor does a child of eight take long to decide which games it likes playing. It is impossible to sell a bad poem to anybody except a literary editor, very few of whom seem to have gone to school; but if we have not let our class down too often before, we shall not have to work too hard to sell a good one. And this brings us to the point.

The problem when choosing material is to find the good single poem. If for any reason one wants to deal with a number of poems in a teaching period, it pays to look for individual poems and to relinquish any idea of finding, say, four poems about fishing, or even four poems that will go well together (whatever that means). Once one has found them, if they *are* good poems, linking them together presents no difficulty.

The single poem is the critical unit, and one had better be very clear about what one should be looking for and where to find it. Let us consider the first point.

To be negative, what sort of poem is it that we do not want to find? Here is the perfect example. I have chosen it because it appears cheerfully in a number of anthologies, and because it seems unsuitable as propaganda for poetry for any age group. It may be a good poem, though I suspect it is not. That is quite beside the point.

### Wattle and Myrtle

Gold of the tangled wilderness of wattle,
Break in the lone green hollows of the hills,
Flame on the iron headlands of the ocean,
Gleam on the margin of the hurrying rills.

## In Particular

Come with thy saffron diadem, and scatter
Odour of Araby that haunts the air;
Queen of the woodland, rival of the roses,
Spring in the yellow tresses of thy hair.

Surely the old Gods, dwellers in Olympus,
Under thy shining loveliness have strayed,
Crowned with thy clusters magical Apollo,
Pan with his reedy music might have played.

Surely within thy fastness Aphrodite,
She of the seaways, fallen from above,
Wandered beneath thy canopy of blossom,
Nothing disdainful of a mortal's love.

Aye, and her sweet breath lingers on the wattle,
Aye, and her myrtle dominates the glade,
And with a deep and perilous enchantment
Melts in the heart of lover and of maid.

JAMES LISTER CUTHBERTSON

First it has a stupid title. This is most important; because a bad title will wreck any poem with a class; just as conversely I have known good titles recommend poems not eminently suitable.

Secondly it is incoherent in general and it lacks sharpness of detail. In other words there is nothing for either the intellect or the imagination to seize upon. Moreover, its idiom is archaic and pretentious, and a bored class will readily find laugh-words in 'myrtle', 'Aphrodite', and 'crowned with thy clusters'. This may seem hard to realize unless one actually has experience, but, in fact, once language becomes opaque a class will very quickly detect in it elements of the ludicrous.

Now let us consider a suitable poem. It is one we all know because quite a large number of people have found it so.

### CARGOES

Quinquireme of Nineveh from distant Ophir
Rowing home to haven in sunny Palestine,
    With a cargo of ivory,
    And apes and peacocks,
Sandalwood, cedarwood, and sweet white wine.

Stately Spanish galleon coming from the Isthmus,
Dipping through the tropics by the palm-green shores,
    With a cargo of diamonds,
    Emeralds, amethysts,
Topazes, and cinnamon, and gold moidores.

Dirty British coaster with a salt-caked smoke-stack
Butting through the Channel in the mad March days,
    With a cargo of Tyne coal,
    Road rail, pig lead,
Firewood, ironware, and cheap tin trays.

JOHN MASEFIELD

This poem has many different excellences, and they are such that each of them appeal to different levels of taste. The nine-year-old enjoys the sound, the eleven-year-old the colour, and the older person the bite, balance and development of the whole thing. Everyone can see what it means; and the only person unlikely to enjoy it is the person who has enjoyed it once and who has now developed what he fondly imagines to be a more recondite taste. For such people education has worked. When a person has reached the stage of sneering at one part of a subject we can tell he is saved and leave his enthusiasms to God.

To say that this is the best or only sort of poem to teach would be nonsense; nor, in spite of its considerable popularity, will it always be successful. It is far from suitable for the infant class; for the grammar school sixth-former it is too obviously clichéd by frequent association.

Yet all good poems for school purposes must share its qualities, or at least combine a considerable proportion of them. Having considered the sort of poem a class is likely to enjoy in general, the teacher needs to look for one that unites these qualities in particular. Such a poem must have, like the Masefield above,

> A clear meaning
> A clearly recognizable mood
> A sound pattern that is functional
> Clear imagery
> Movement and cohesion

Considered in abstract these are very simple requirements. They are very often hard to meet, however, and they are quite certainly essential.

We have all experienced the lesson in which a smug-faced teacher has had to explain the meaning of a poem. 'What does it mean, Smith?' 'Tell him, Jones!' 'Oh well, I can see I shall have to explain it myself.' The wider implications of such an attitude can be allowed to pass. Its effect on the class is not so easy to overlook. First the class comes to feel that poetry is something that has to be explained, and therefore to consider that reading it is an activity only suitable for school. Second, there is a growing feeling of exasperation when so many of the explanations turn out to be trite or merely woolly. 'Prose is straightforward; Poetry is not'—pleasure and purpose die with that conviction.

A wrong choice in particular cannot afford to be misunderstood. The prompt class conviction that a certain poem is a dud does nothing to hinder the swing of a lesson. If the teacher has to spend ten minutes explaining a wrong choice, on the other hand, a tremendous amount of energy and enthusiasm is dissipated on both sides. Therefore the poem must have, above anything else, a clear meaning.

There are occasions when prosaic clarity is not enough. If, for example, the idea is incapable of being grasped by the class, then its clear expression will not really avail one. Again, statements that seem extraordinarily obvious to the teacher because of a wider background of reading are quite incomprehensible to some classes. As teacher one is often slow to recognize the change from vocabulary common to prose and poetry alike to vocabulary more generally current in poetry. For example, a class can enter quite a simple couplet with interest and lose themselves for ever.

> A dozen ponies by the willows stood
> And watched their image dying in the flood.

'Image' and 'flood' are points of simple difficulty. 'When did the poet say there was a flood? I thought this poem was called "Drought"!' is quite a fair comment. If they do not understand 'image', and it is a word of vague as well as varied association, then they will not understand 'dying'. The pupil who suggested to me that this couplet meant that the horses watched their foals drowning was being far from stupid.

One more word: 'clear meaning' must be considered in conjunction with the medium of presentation. If one suddenly recites to a class, without preamble, the lines

> 'Lars Porsena of Clusium'

or

> 'In Xanadu did Kubla Khan'

one had just as well be talking in Turkish. The ear is a strange organ. Again, whole poems can hinge upon simple points about which the *listener* will be perpetually in doubt.

## In Particular

'O (Son or Sun?)' he said, 'you came today
   And you will come tomorrow;
And if you stay a day away
   The day will start in sorrow.'

and does 'a day away' mean 'away a day' or a day's distance away? There are many similar instances: 'Ploughman's gait' can seem 'ploughman's gate', 'Eve's fatal bough' suggests her opening night in Eden; and if one is foolish enough to offer up those phrases which are not only ambiguous but comically so, like 'wild woodbine' and 'watery bier', one asks for what one gets. I still remember the young teacher who read us Francis Thompson's

> She gave me tokens three:
> A look, a kiss of her winsome mouth,
> And a wild raspberry

and of the other one who took that delightful line of Milton's, which incidentally touched off much mirth,

> A thousand foreskins fell, the flower of Palestine

and tried to decide whether 'foreskins' were synecdoches or metonymies.

This leads us rather to the next point: A poem must possess a clearly recognizable mood. Mood is most important. It is essential that a class should know immediately what sort of effect a poem is aiming at. Indecision, especially in achieving the melodramatic or the fanciful (both rich fields for exploration), always results in embarrassment or laughter. A comic poem should be equally unequivocal in its approach; the teacher should always seek one with a decisive opening line. In the case of parody, unless it is also funny in its own right, the class should always be well acquainted with what is being parodied. On the other hand it never does to read a poem merely to introduce its parody. Parody, like any other form of satirical imitation, demands its own rightful context. Its target should be familiar in detail.

Mood is always at the mercy of clarity, and it can be ruined by any of the ambiguities noted above. It can also be marred by a hundred and one things which it is rarely considered decorous for an adult to notice, but which he had better heed if he is a teacher.

For example, I said earlier that one should avoid any idea of 'otherness', any feeling that poetry is the product of the extraordinary. Here are some names as set out in a well-known anthology: Felicia Dorothea Hemans, Denys Lefebvre, Arthur Hugh Clough, James Lister Cuthbertson, John Greenleaf Whittier, and Osbert Sitwell. Children quick to deride one another's names will be no less vicious at the expense of the Percy Bysshes, the Dante Gabriels, the Rudyards and the Coventrys. Obviously one cannot veto poetry just because it is produced by people with names that do not sort well with a brick-street context. But one can at least keep any mention of a poet's name down to surname plus initials, if it seems to offer undesirable elements. The whole question of how much the class need be aware of a poetic personality is a very open one; and it is often unnecessary to mention the poet's name at all. What has to be avoided at all cost is the preparatory chill that descends if one is foolish enough to announce something like ' "Dumb Friends" by Cuthbert Lushington'. Mood is destroyed before the poem itself has any chance of creating it. There is no need here to list the sort of titles that cause trouble. It should be remembered in dealing with a less intelligent form that almost anything that sounds unusual will be badly received.

The third requirement was a functional rhythm. It must be emphasized that one's definition of 'functional' depends primarily upon the age of the class. Sounds that to an older

child would seem gross and unnatural are not only tolerable
but desirable to children of five and six. To them the

> Yicketty
> Yacketty
> Riggledy raggledy
> Rasp of the Rajah's beard

is a thoroughly admirable sound. To them verse is something
positive, and entirely to be preferred to prose.

Older children like verse to be unobtrusive; but until they
are about ten or eleven years old they are quite prepared for
it to be noisily functional at times. 'How They Brought the
Good News', which in many respects is not ideal, always
seems to succeed with children of this age because of its fine
galloping rhythm.

During their early teens it is quite wrong to make them
observe the pattern of a poem. In a rhyming poem they are
generally observant about rhyme itself, often critically so.
Although some bad critical criteria may be involved, it
should be realized that most people unacquainted with the
actual form of poetry (e.g. most children of twelve, thirteen,
and fourteen, and most adults making a serious study of Eng-
lish for the first time) like their rhymes to rhyme. Half-
rhymes, eye-rhymes, difficult rhymes like many of Brown-
ing's (save when one is dealing with comic poems) are best
avoided. Bad rhyme is the first target of the naïve, but
maturing, critical intelligence.

Such an insistence on formal virtues need not be taken to
mean that blank or free verse is undesirable in the classroom.
Quite the reverse. It has been suggested to me by many pupils
that blank verse is preferable to rhyming verse for telling
stories; and if the formal distinction between verse and
prose is avoided, free verse is often a most desirable medium.
After all, much of the best verse written by children of

eleven, twelve, and thirteen is free. D. H. Lawrence's 'The Snake' is a very successful poem with a wide range of age groups, from twelve-year-olds upwards. The child can see the functional nature of much of its technique.

Clear imagery is something far more difficult to obtain, largely because the adult approach to imagery is more reasoned than a child's, though rarely so reasonable.

In children's own work the images are frequent and immediate. This is because they *are* images, they *are* visual; they represent an immediate fusing of two objects, uncomplicated by convention, unworried by any possible charge of plagiarism. That is, they contain no trace of the conceit.

Adult imagery is often less immediate, not only because the image is adulterated by these latter elements, but because it is reflective, and goes beyond the visual to marry object with idea.

The development from one state of mind to the other is neither simple nor consistent. At the risk of seeming too glib, I would like to suggest that there are three main stages. The ages are, of course, very approximate; they would fluctuate considerably according to intelligence and educational environment. If we take the nursery rhyme as our point of departure and the adult taste in poetry as our somewhat dispersed area of arrival, we shall find between them these instances of transition:

9–12: A liking for direct (mainly visual) image.
12–15: A preference for no images at all, other than that conjured up by words of immediate association.
Likely to be encountered at any time after thirteen: An addiction to images that 'work out' logically.

Thus the first stage is the more vital and exciting, for both word and image are living experiences. The second stage, educationally, is the attempt to cushion the shock occasioned by the death of those experiences. The third stage is when the mind forces itself to re-experience intellectually, and to prepare itself for the adult stage, which is when the mind recollects, but does not realize that memory is enriched by the artifice of remembering.

This phenomenon of the maturing response to the image is typical of the mind's changing approach to poetry in general; but it does bring the problem rather more clearly before us: at some stage, approximately in the thirteenth year, the mind rejects nearly everything artistic that it previously embraced. It first purges; then it logicizes. The teacher, unless he is going to do irreparable harm to his cause, must react quickly to this moment of change. The imagination dies overnight and the intellect is reborn.

There is an attendant danger: that is the closeness of the truly juvenile and the truly adult experience. They speak the same language but they do not understand one another. Too frequently literature written for children by adults, or deemed suitable for children by adults, is in fact totally unsuitable. A supreme example of this is the nonsense verse of Edward Lear, a retrospective joy for most people.

Nonsense verse—which is in a sense limited by being its own image—is difficult in the classroom, though it often succeeds with the individual child. The reason is that it is an imaginative pastiche: it is conceived by that part of the adult mind which is close to the child, but inevitably its idiom is over-sophisticated.

T. S. Eliot's 'Possum' poems are works which suffer in this way, magnificent though several of them are. In almost any classroom context their central image would be wrong. 'Cats with character' is an idea that appeals only to the mature or the very young; but the poems' idioms and peripheral humours prevent them from being used with the very young, just as the subject disqualifies them with intermediate age groups. They can succeed with young teenagers, of course, but an essential ingredient of such classroom success is a conviction on the part of the whole class that they are not being 'got at' intellectually. In a poetry lesson it is hard to persuade them of this.

For the single child, or for the small group of older pupils in the private school, one can choose more recklessly. The individual is only hampered from within: the pupil in a class of forty has thirty-nine hindrances outside himself; and of that forty one violent reaction on the part of any one can include the others within a second. The young are preyed upon by the self-confidence of their fellows. A lesson can founder upon a single inadequate note.

Hence philosophizing and the pointing of morals do not make for success, for to the child they represent opaque elements in a transparent idiom through which he fancies he can glimpse reality. 'The poet describes the old bridge, and then goes on to wonder how much water has passed under it since he was a boy'—a poem needing any such explanation always augments the pupil's suspicions that poets think too much and their thoughts are just a trifle arbitrary. The poem must not wander away from its image. It must have cohesion.

Yet it must have movement. A narrative poem obviously moves, and if the narrative is arresting then it meets all of the necessary requirements; but it is not always realized that a descriptive poem must have the same sense of movement. Pastoral, with its multilateral deployment of image, its addition of leaf to tree and tree to wood, is never suitable. What is needed is a strong central picture—a man, an aeroplane, a factory, a waterfall—around which the mind can progress.

As a belated text here are some extracts from examination essays written by pupils long addicted to complete cultural honesty. Their ages are fourteen and fifteen. Considered with

the more youthful manifestoes given elsewhere they present
a fairly coherent picture:

> 'I like my poems to tell a story. . . .'
> 'I like poems to be funny. . . .'
> 'Perhaps it's not great verse but I enjoyed it.'
> 'I do not like those poems which are all very nice, but
> do not leave you any better off. . . .'
> 'I prefer them to be written in modern language. . . .'
> 'They should not for example have names like Cedric
> Snodgrass.'
> 'fiery short pieces of description'
> 'They should be rhymed with sensible words'
> 'no similes, especially homeric similes. . .'

They all boggled at any poetry that needed to be 'taught'
or 'explained'. Educated to worship a Muse who wore corsets,
I envy them their lack of jargon.

Having said so much about texture it may seem a little
obvious to add remarks about subject; but this is something
on which very clear guidance can be given; and as a result of
it an inexperienced teacher will find his field agreeably
limited.

As a good general rule, any poem that is a character study
will succeed. It does not matter whether it is objective or
subjective, ancient or modern, providing it is reasonably
short. The symbol will change according to age: from Gnome
to Knight and then to Postman or Sailor in the primary
school, for example; from man dramatic, to man comic, to
man rational in the secondary school; but its central appeal
will remain constant. Jack Sprat, Sir Nickety, Wordsworth's
Leechgatherer, even Yeats' Irish Airman, are all aspects of
the acceptable symbol of man.

Woman, to make what at first seems a nice distinction, is
rarely part of this symbol. At best she is stylized in verse; and

the wild wet women of Romantic poetry are lacking in appeal for boys and girls alike.

Nor can one recommend the poem which becomes a character-study only by that gross impersonation known as personification. 'Time, the old gypsyman' is rarely entreated to stay, hence, one suspects, his eager progress through anthology after anthology. Two years ago he halted his caravan fleetingly in a G.C.E. paper.

The personification of animals is an exception. Pupils until the age of twelve enjoy poems that personalize the entire alphabet of the bestiary. Tortoises in doggerel are always preferable to maidens in moated granges, mourning, or mink; and quite certainly better than abstractions with scythes.

Comic characters are usually very successful; though in this case it is better to select the comedy rather than the character with reference to the age of the pupils. 'Tim Turpin' by Hood, 'Bloudy Jack' (in an edited form) by Barhum, and several of the sharper Bab characters, together with the por-traiture of artists as different as Hilaire Belloc and Cyril Fletcher, make excellent fare.

The one character that the pupil hopes to be spared is the poet himself. Wordsworth's 'Daffodils' fails in class not because it is about daffodils but because it is about Words-worth, who was a pretty dull dog.

This leads us to the next point: if the poem is not focused on character, one must be careful that it is not a transparency with the poet himself appearing as a sort of anaemic montage in the foreground. For teenage classes the poet can only exist satisfactorily if he is also another symbol: soldier in the case of Sassoon, Owen, and Keith Douglas, cragsman in the case of Winthrop Young, and so forth. By 'exist' I mean exist in the poem. The fact that the poet often is another symbol in real life will, if insisted on, sunder poetry and reality even more disastrously. Sir Philip Sydney's glorious end, Raleigh's varied pageant, are rich subjects in themselves but poor introductions to their poetry. For the modern boy there is no relationship between the proffered flask of water and the sonnets to Stella. A poet may perhaps be a successful symbol in his poetry if he appear modern; but in truth there is not one poetic attitude of Auden, Spender, Eliot or Day-Lewis likely to recommend them in class, though in 'Old Possum's Book of Practical Cats', 'The Night Mail', 'Landscape Near an Aerodrome', and 'The Flight' each has produced objective poetry that is eminently suitable.

So much for the elimination of the ego. What of the object? Ships, trains, planes, these are sound subjects. So are buses, fish-shops, fairs and other less likely tangibles. What one aims at is a hard bright image, a sharp vocabulary, a sheer movement, and unadulterated attitude, in description; and in narrative, progress, order, and climax. These can be found in the comic and some of the heroic poetry of the nineteenth century and in the descriptive poetry of the twentieth. One will need to endure much in order to find little unless one wields the wand of divination. The best advice is to look for a laugh or a story for any age between ten and sixteen. After that one must seek poetry, and that is hard to find.

The infant class has a fair range of material ready to hand; and the problem is not so much to discover how much of it to utilize as to decide when to reject it in its entirety. Bearing in mind the remarks above one can range widely or narrowly among the material designed for the *reading* and *comprehension* ability of this resilient age; though one's worry is for future damage rather than present discontent. Some infant poems are horridly sentimental, however. Avoid these and their lady anthologists. I have seen a poem bring tears to a child's eyes—indeed I can remember even now a verse that made me cry at the age of six. Unfortunately the child remembers its own sentimentalism with resentment. If a playmate catches sight of those tears the teacher has perpetuated a major educational blunder.

A really excellent area of exploration, varied and comprehensive, is the nursery-rhyme. The 'cruelty' of some of these does little damage, and their intellectual inconsistency is admirably countered by their imaginative integrity. The teacher should add two books in particular to his private or public shelf: *The Oxford Dictionary of Nursery Rhymes* and *The Oxford Nursery Rhyme Book*. The latter is specially valuable as it has a bold type-face and is pleasingly illustrated. Its format is most agreeable from the child's point of view, and it contains enough material by itself to carry the pupil past these specialized years.

So much for where. Now for what.

For the infant and first junior years, wordplay such as:

> Three little ghostesses,
> Sitting on postesses,
> Eating buttered toastesses,
> Greasing their fistesses,
> Up to their wristesses.
> Oh, what beastesses
> To make such feastesses.

Characters, such as:

> Robin the Bobbin,
> the big-bellied Ben,
> He ate more meat
> than fourscore men;
> He ate a cow,
> he ate a calf,
> He ate a butcher
> and a half,
> He ate a church

> he ate a steeple,
> He ate a priest
> and all the people!
> A cow and a calf,
> An ox and a half,
> A church and a steeple,
> And all the good people,
> And yet he complained
> that his stomach wasn't full

Certain jolly humours, such as:

> Peter Piper picked a peck of pickled pepper;
> A peck of pickled pepper Peter Piper picked.
> If Peter Piper picked a peck of pickled pepper,
> Where's the peck of pickled pepper Peter Piper
> picked.

Where these cannot be read, they are all brief enough to be learned from recitation. When the child can read, compulsory learning is dangerous; but at the infant stage very much can be learned willingly, and upon how much of value is learnt the child's future progress depends. Jingles learnt in childhood stimulate the imagination for ever.

Therefore one should increase the child's counting rhymes —those usual for playground games—as much as possible. The triumphant chanting of unusual sounds, in and out of the classroom, is a most useful practice.

> Inter, mitzy, titzy, tool,
> Ira, dira, domina,
> Oker, poker, dominoker,
> Out goes you.

The complete performance of 'The House that Jack Built' has a useful exhaustion quotient, as well as being a brain-stretcher. Besides, if the child enjoys playing with sound now, he will more easily understand sound patterns later.

One should include useful (or pseudo-useful) rhymes. 'Thirty Days hath September' is not the only one. There is the whole realm of weather lore, and not just 'Red Sky at Night':

> Mackerel sky,
> Mackerel sky,
> Not long wet,
> Not long dry.

Even the order of Kings:

> First William the Norman,
> Then William his son,
> Henry, Stephen, and Henry,
> Then Richard and John,
>                    etc.

With pupils a few years older who have learnt the value of mnemonics, one can encourage the composition of useful ones. I thought this a couth example:

> When do you use a metaphor.
> O dear, I am not sure.
> Why use a simile.
> For saying 'a' is like to 'b'.

While the mind is so receptive it is convenient to offer it these utilitarian verses. The mature mind recalls such jingles with affection, as well as with a surge of gratitude for the useful mnemonic. If literature is to succeed with the child later it is imperative that these primitive rhythmic patterns should progress now. It is a fact that many of the secondary school pupils most hostile to poetry have not learned any at their primary school, sorry though this is.

Once beyond infancy the child becomes a thrall to the teacher's energy and discretion. The material does not come so readily to hand.

The right sort of book to search in is the private one which contains poems that one has to 'present' to the pupil by means more adventurous than the printed page. These years, from eight to eleven, are the ones for the 'set poetry lesson' as we saw in the last chapter. Very little can go wrong here—I've seen a class of nine-year-olds survive *The Ancient Mariner*; but there is one caution. Such is the general receptiveness of this age-group that the emotional comes over very clearly. To subject a class to painful experiences imaginatively is only to store up resentment for later. A ludicrous account of torment is safe enough:

> They are twisting your right leg Nor-West,
>     And your left leg due South,
>     And your knee's in your mouth,
> And your head is poked on your breast,
>                 And it's prest,
> I protest, almost into your chest!

but an eight-year-old mind—and even sometimes a ten-year-old—recoils from such images as

> With beetles placed in walnut shells
> Deprived her child of sight.

ridiculous though they appear to a more mature intelligence; and when the maturing mind exorcises its horrors it can also cast out the poetry that introduced them.

The specially prepared school book is still useful for this age; but already one encounters less single-minded collections. Publishers have looked for a wider market, and the resultant symposia are to be indulged in with due care. Some of the *Weekend Books* have contained excellent material for this age, however. De la Mare, both in *Collected Poems* and in *Collected Rhymes and Verses* is a very rich source; even when his work fails to provide a suitable subject it always has a sharp idiom. Kipling has much about him: his fine poem on the smugglers is a sure success. Masefield, Belloc, and lesser poets like Hodgson and Gibson, offer considerable store; their imaginations are not unduly complex and their eyes are clear.

These are highways, and at the very start of the chapter I made it clear that it is the byways that count. The good teacher will always be looking elsewhere: through those interminable—but unjustly neglected—nineteenth-century comic collections, through nineteenth-century collections in general looking for 'characters', and—best of all—through the early collections of street ballads. The text is never sacred, and the teacher *must* sophisticate. Harden the heart, and one can truncate much Gilbert and some Barhum to suitable dimensions. Cut, edit; purge and burn. It is not poetry one wishes to present but a liking for poetry. Therefore whatever is liked must be *called* poetry.

At this age the imagination becomes less gentle and starts to lurk like a wild beast in its environmental jungle. If the class comes from homes full of books, well enough. More than likely, much more than likely, it emerges from tall tenements, or ordinary houses that do their honest best to be the same as their neighbours. You may have to applaud the chaster quatrains from *Reveille*, or the doggerel imbecilities of those crude Sunday papers that offer a diminutive quantity of verse, generally penned by someone incapable of writing prose. One concession to folk culture the child will not make, however: Patience Strong and her coterie are never accepted. And woe betide the teacher of girls who thinks that the verses in women's magazines are a point of departure. That, too, has been tried.

For the eleven- and twelve-year-olds one wants to cast prescribed selections overboard. There are a number of poems that they must at least hear well read, in addition to their creative work. One should always seek to enrich this list but there is no need to enlarge it unduly. Poems of varied interest such as: 'The Ballad of the Revenge', 'John Gilpin', 'The Rhyme of the Nancy Bell', 'Tim Turpin', and 'Drake's Drum', are well worth tackling now, while the pupils are new to school and at a receptive age. It is valuable to build up a heroic conception of poetry while one can; if one keeps away from the sentimental or wildly unrealistic the pupil will remember this period with affection. Quite frequently pupils who come to dislike poetry because of subsequent bad teaching recall the poems they have read at this age, and say, 'If only poetry could all be like that'. One must make what one can of the time at one's disposal; but the seeds of boredom are scattered as one sows the wildest delight. The ideal is not quite to give a class as much poetry as it wants. To be sparing ensures a less-jaded response in the future. If one has to stock an anthology (and heaven forbid it should be one's only resource) 'Smith' still has much to recommend him. *The Poet's Window*—a great favourite—contains, like all anthologies, some good among much bad, and it is also impertinent enough to pretend it is graded in four volumes according to age. If you can use all these volumes with your eleven-year-olds, use them—it will repay buying. If not, do not use it at all. However, anthologies are the lazy man's answer, and poetry must not be taught by lazy men.

It is for the ages thirteen, fourteen, and fifteen, that the greatest single emphasis must be placed on material. These ages can be involved in nothing except laughter, and an especially non-brittle type of violence that invokes laughter. The perfect sort of poem is:

*Material*



### BILLY THE KID

Billy was a bad man
And carried a big gun;
He was always after greasers
And kept 'em on the run.

He shot one every morning
For to make his morning meal.
And let a white man sass him,
He was sure to feel his steel.

He kept folks in hot water,
And he stole from many a stage;
And when he was full of liquor
He was always in a rage.

But one day he met a man
Who was a whole lot badder.
And now he's dead,
And we ain't none the sadder.

One can find such poems in the works of Robert Service (sometimes), and in the Canadian national poets in general; in American folk poetry, to which the Alan Lomax books on the North American ballad are the best introduction, but to which any skiffle broadsheet will add much; and in scattered form in the very many books of Victorian street ballads, execution broadsheets, etc. When one is dealing with this absolutely 'real' material, background-type introductions are permissible. Eighteenth-century issues of the *Gentleman's Magazine* contain suitable prose horrors to support the execution broadsheets, and one can obtain ample prose (and verse) amplification of the Wild West in the many semi-factual North American histories. A library that deals with the real instead of the fictional Wild West is worth cultivating, and the enterprising teacher can either draw up his own private bibliography or, better, his own scrapbook. The class will co-operate in this sort of 'research'. After reading a lurid account of 'the battle of the store' in a strangely illiterate book entitled *Arizona's Dark and Bloody Land*, it was easy to persuade a skiffle addict to find the same story in the ballad of 'Jesse Owen'. The class preferred the ballad.

Suitable humour is more easy to find and, on the whole, even more successful. Humour has variety; violence is monotonous, and it certainly does no harm to let a class be aware of this. The Penguin *Comic and Curious Verse*, the Penguin *More Comic and Curious Verse*, *The Faber Book of Comic Verse*, *The Oxford Book of Light Verse* (in general too mature), the Faber *Verse and Worse* by Arnold Silcock; *The 'Bab' Ballads*, *The Ingoldsby Legends*, *The Collected Poems of Hood*, the various publications of Ogden Nash and Don Marquis, together with the vast number of possible excursions into digests, magazines, annuals, holiday books—all these, as the tortoise said, are a start.

With pupils of this age one should capitalize discontent as cunningly as possible. Tennyson's *Morte D'Arthur*, for example, always holds attention; but the absence of realism, implied in 'the knightly growth' and the threats of the wounded king, causes an increasing stir of adverse comment. This is time for William Morris's 'The Haystack in the Floods'. The class responds to the contrasting view of chivalry:

> . . . 'his hand
> In Robert's hair; she saw him send
> The thin steel down; the blow told well,
> Right backward the knight Robert fell,
> And moaned as dogs do, being half-dead,

> Unwitting, as I deem: so then
> Godmar turned grinning to his men,
> Who ran, some five or six, and beat
> His head to pieces at their feet.'

'The War Song of Dinas Vawr' becomes a convenient antidote to 'Sir Galahad'.

Perhaps for the only time, the teacher is dealing with some sort of 'chain reaction'. He can therefore afford to ignore the doctrine of the single poem, and offer rough-and-ready single-topic symposiums. With a really good fifteen-year-old class it is possible to be quite adventurous: Herbert Read's 'Bombing Casualties in Spain', Wilfred Owen's 'Dulce et Decorum Est', C. Day Lewis's 'Assertion', for example. A tried and trusty programme with less responsive classes is my 'eight o'clock walk' symposium, consisting of Housman's three poems on hanging, a few appropriate verses from 'The Widow in the Bye Street', 'Villon's Straight Tip to All Cross Coves', and 'The Faking Boy'. This last is not well known and is worth printing entire. Edited to avoid trouble it reads:

> The faking boy to the trap is gone,
> At the nubbing chit you'll find him;
> The hempen cord they have girded on,
> And his elbows pinned behind him.
> 'Smash my glim!' cries the reg'lar card,
> 'Though the girl you love betrays you,
> Don't split, but die both game and hard,
> And grateful pals shall praise you!'
>
> The bolt it fell—a jerk, a strain!
> The sheriffs fled asunder;
> The faking boy ne'er spoke again,
> For they pulled his legs from under.
> And there he dangled on the tree,

> That soul of love and bravery!
> Oh, that such men should victims be
> Of law, and law's vile knavery!

Obviously such lessons are susceptible of a creative follow up.
After Henley's

> Suppose you screeve? or go cheap-jack?
> Or fake the broads? or fig a nag?
> Or thimble rig? or knap a yack?
> Or pitch a snide? or smack a rag?

one can invite a similar composition with real or faked
modern criminal slang. The class generally knows this only
too well, and to create verse from 'bull', 'twirl', 'screw', etc.,
makes them receptive to further literary excursions into
quasi-reality. One can find in Mayhew as much nineteenth-
century criminal slang as one can use. The pupils have their
own sources for more modern usages.

For this age, too, one should always be on the look-out for
the unusual versicle. Skiffle and calypso rhymes are easy to
obtain, but they need to be reinforced by quantities of gambit
material, such as the doleful ditty that alliterates the alpha-
betical woes of the Austrian Army, or the letter pun poem
that starts

> Sad nymphs of UL, U have much to cry for,
> Sweet MLE K U never more shall C!
> O SX Maids! come hither and D,O,
> With tearful I, this MT LEG.

Ideally this process should have started earlier, but its continu-
ance now is imperative. It is a pity that school teachers cannot
provide pupils with adult smoking-concert material. If they
could, poetry would benefit immensely. Since they cannot
they must supply the best possible substitutes. Once more, the

success of such material depends on the extent to which it can be reinforced by the pupil's own creative work.

Much that I have recommended is not great poetry. Nor should one seek to present great poetry in school unless it admirably fulfils other more important educational conditions. It is only in the senior school—if then—that one reads great novels, for example, and poetry needs a far more oblique approach than the novel. The child should be provided with verse that will interest him.

Whenever I am able to use this approach exclusively, up to sixth-form standard, a very interesting fact arises: when we turn to significant as distinct from light verse there is a clear preference for contemporary poetry. This is entirely as it should be. The pupil has been led, creatively, to a point where he is willing to sympathize with what is being created around him. He is more alive to the mature idiom of today than he is to that of yesterday. But from today he turns willingly to yesterday to find what it still has to offer. He accepts dead idioms, stale usages, conventionalized phrases as what they are, as a glass wherein he can see other men's reality. Had he been educated chronologically, however, he would have come to equate poetry with archaism and pretence, and if he had accepted it he would have turned to today with prejudice.

Everything one does, every poem one chooses, should be chosen to enlarge the pupil's sense of enjoyment. The young pupil must be encouraged to celebrate the poem, the older pupil the life in the poem.

When we exploit his interest historically, we should look for that portion of the past that is most alive. It should be remembered that poets like Milton, Pope, and Dryden, however much they appeal to a mature taste, seem, to the uninitiated, quite dead. Given time, greatness declares itself. We must not be its too insistent advocate.

# 8. CHORAL SPEAKING

CHORAL SPEECH is an essential of good poetry teaching. Yet it is not merely a part of 'Method', but an activity in its own right, demanding considerable invention from teacher and class, and repaying their efforts in a most satisfying manner. Handled properly it gratifies the creative, dramatic, and even the exhibitionist, tendencies which most of us possess; and at the same time it gives deep insights into individual poems and impresses them effortlessly upon the memory. It has nearly all the educational and many of the cultural advantages of drama, while requiring far less time and space. Where it flourishes, poetry will flourish; yet to succeed with it the teacher needs only an average competence in the classroom. Indecision on the part of the teacher and self-consciousness on the part of the class are the only two factors likely to impede success; good preparation can do away with one and familiarity will eliminate the other. Habit makes it acceptable to all age groups if *the material is well chosen*; but it is difficult to introduce for the first time to thirteen-, fourteen-, and fifteen-year-olds, and it should not be attempted with pupils of this age unless they already enjoy it, or unless they are very responsive to other forms of dramatic activity.

There are two main approaches to choral speech, the 'tonal' and the 'dramatic'. Which is employed in the case of a given poem depends upon the poem itself. Ideally, with an adult group, one chooses a work that gives scope for both approaches; indeed, in practice it would be difficult to find a poem that calls exclusively for one or the other. What one generally does in the classroom, however, is to encourage a preponderance of the most convenient method. For younger forms, for the less enthusiastic or the less practised class, or in cases where quick results are required, this is undoubtedly the dramatic. The tonal approach is largely the province of the mature and the expert. Yet because it is a rehearsed activity, it frequently features in more public contexts: at speech-day or on the competition platform; and for that reason I treat it at length. With patience the very young can be coaxed to perform great things; but it should be remembered that their value should be assessed educationally rather than aesthetically.

Now to definitions: By a 'dramatic' approach I mean the attempt to isolate by means of individual voices or individualized groups of voices the different characters in, or characteristics of, a poem. There are great chances here for the exercise of personal gifts, and interpretation generally becomes enlarged as the different performers make more and more suggestions for improvement.

By 'tonal' approach, on the other hand, I mean this: the poem as a whole is conceived as a choric entity, and the voices of the group are regarded as instruments for the transmission of sound. They are variously permutated, but the whole owes its effect to rehearsed and concerted effort. It emerges symphonically rather than dramatically.

To give a simple example: Swinburne's 'When the Hounds of Spring' would call for a tonal approach, whereas Auden's 'O What is That Sound' would call for a dramatic approach. Almost any chorus from a classical-type drama would call for a combination of the two.

There is a further Aristotelean subdivision: the teacher can aim for an immediate or a rehearsed effect. He can seek to *present* the poem by means of choral speech, or he can seek to *perpetuate* it. Paradoxically it is the immediate effect that requires more preparation; and the only real preparation this requires is forethought.

I have expressed it like that because it seems to me desirable to destroy the fallacy of the choral-speaking expert. A great deal of nonsense has been written about choral speech; it is unpleasant enough to discover that many of its exponents regard it as a difficult art, as the sort of activity concerning which an intelligent teacher ought to attend a course before attempting to teach it; but there are greater evils.

To present a group with a score which aims at preconceived effects seems to me educationally indefensible as well as artistically unsound. A teacher who controls an activity is inviting boredom in direct proportion to the extent to which he frustrates creation; that is—absolutely. So if one aims at a rehearsed effect, one should start with only a rough plan and allow circumstances during rehearsal to enrich it; in this way the individual pupil does not start off with the dismal certainty that all he has to do is improve on what he is doing. Instead of attending a course all the teacher need do is start his pupils working and listen to them; then sculpt in sound, taking good care that individual members of the class are allowed their turn with the hammer.

If this essential point is grasped and accepted by the reader, that choral speaking is an act of group creation in which the invention will be found to be spontaneous, just like other creative work in poetry when it is properly encouraged; in other words, if it is seen that here as elsewhere successful English teaching is a matter of catalytic self-effacement, then there is really no need to read any further in this chapter. However, most people like to provide themselves with a chart of an unknown area. In offering one, I would like to record that the natives are friendly.

## Choral Speaking

First, to illustrate the two main methods by means of the finished product.

### The Dramatic Method

Here is a well-known chorus by W. H. Auden:

At last the secret is out, as it always must come in the end,
The delicious story is ripe to tell to the intimate friend;
Over the tea-cups and in the square the tongue has its desire;
Still waters run deep, my dear, there's never smoke without
    fire.

Behind the corpse in the reservoir, behind the ghost on the
    links,
Behind the lady who dances and the man who madly drinks,
Under the look of fatigue, the attack of migraine and the sigh
There is always another story, there is more than meets the eye.

For the clear voice suddenly singing, high up in the convent
    wall,
The scent of elder bushes, the sporting prints in the hall,
The croquet matches in summer, the handshake, the cough,
    the kiss,
There is always a wicked secret, a private reason for this.

As one reads it, one is immediately aware of its suitability for the dramatic method: it is simple in meaning, direct in its associations, and possesses easily grasped images, marshalled in short uncomplicated speech units. In other words it presents no rhythmic, imaginative, or syntactic problems to the reader or the listener. On the other hand, there are no lines that merit any strong vocal reinforcement; no barrages of sound produced by the frequent discharge of organ vowels; no real tonal crescendoes or diminuendoes; no flaunted alliterations or onomatopoeias inviting a whole orchestra of tongues used separately and in unison.

Again, it is not merely a poem *suitable* for the dramatic method; it *shouts* dramatic method aloud; it suggests how it should be performed, and it is obvious that the method will enrich the poem. The short speech units imply differing characteristics, 'the look of fatigue', and 'the attack of migraine' or 'the scent of elder bushes' and 'the sporting prints in the hall'; and differing characters, 'the lady who dances', and 'the man who madly drinks'. The 'sigh', 'the handshake', 'the cough' and 'the kiss' are all words that call for an individual performance by an individual voice or individualized group of voices. The sigh is wistful, the handshake hearty, the cough sepulchral, the kiss tender, yearning, arch, or what you will. That is the first consideration, the diversity of possibilities. The second is the obvious *unity* of some of the characteristics: 'the intimate friend', 'the sigh', 'the kiss', for example, suggest a character, a single voice that will come in at the right moment; those few words represent a part to play, and endless subtleties of sound to rehearse.

Once one starts weaving a tapestry the class responds quickly. The process is humorous, and there is no single answer. Does 'the man who madly drinks' experience for his sins 'the attack of migraine', does he merely offer a panged cough or does he recover enough to recall heartily, or with dissipated listlessness, 'the sporting prints in the hall'? Does he gather himself up for a 'handshake', or is it his own voice, as he stumbles past innumerable pink elephants, that uncovers the horrors of 'the ghost on the links', suggesting a sort of alcoholic trance at the dread stroke of twelve?

My own answer would be withheld until I knew the group concerned. And once the group knew me they would realize that it would be *their* answer, and not mine, that would be given finality. The poem would be played with. In another chapter I said that no poem, formally presented, is worth a period's work; but a choral experience becomes far more than mere poem. Can one member gargle even more grimly in damnation's ink to produce 'the corpse in the reservoir'; can another suggest 'the scent of the elder bushes' beneath his offended nose with even greater distaste?

Time can be happily spent, for frequently the whole group will explode with laughter at someone's vocal excesses or someone else's vocal cramps. As individuals become more confident it will be seen that they start to gesticulate and mime their way through their lines. One receives a tremendous feeling of exuberance when this method is successfully used.

The advantages are many: in addition to dramatic expression and voice practice, and above all the rare illusion that the class has done something physical in an English lesson, pupils come to know and enjoy a poem without ever being made to learn it. They also come to see the same sort of excellences in other poems; and to read poetry aloud with far more gusto.

When one has reached the happy state in which normal class reading can be encouraged to twitter or boom without embarrassment one is very close to all-round victory. But even if class proficiency remains low, and it rarely does, one has at one's disposal a number of techniques left over from choral speech when one wishes to present a poem spontaneously.

For example, one can take a poem similar to the one above and preselect the voices: 'A will read this, B will read that, then A and B will read this line together and we will all come in with the refrain.' A new poem can be presented in this way, repeated for added polish, and the lesson can pass on. The class will have become accustomed to this technique and perform without embarrassment.

Similarly in a more complicated or adult poem that has a dramatic content, for example the *Rime of the Ancient Mariner*:

A will be the narrator, B the Ancient Mariner, and C the wedding guest on a normal reading through. Better still, one can score the whole poem for single voice effects. The first description of the Albatross has its own ominous voice, the sun symbol its hearty exponent throughout the poem, the moon its calculating chill note, and so on.

Indeed, with many less able forms I cast the dignity of the poem temporarily to the winds. I have even had a whole crew of mariners speak through their Ancient's voice:

> *A:*  The ship was cheered,
> *B:*                               the harbour cleared,
> *C:*  Merrily did we drop
> *D:*  Below the kirk,
> *E:*                       below the hill,
> *F:*  Below the lighthouse top.

Great Art is never harmed by laughter, and laughter is often one of the best ways of exorcizing the mental discomforts the greatest art occasions. Most teenage classes find things to laugh at in *The Ancient Mariner*. It is best to stimulate laughter first so that they turn happily to the poem, rather than risk the poem provoking their derision unaided.

The tonal method, although it offers the individual less opportunities for self-expression, should also be approached as a creative activity. Upon how genuinely creative it becomes will largely depend its interest and value to the class. If I seem less happy about it, it is not because it is undesirable or difficult, but because it can only flourish properly when conditions are appropriate, and these depend very much upon the degree to which class inventiveness has been stimulated by other methods. There is also a great temptation for public choral speaking to be completely tonal. People expect it. The sensible teacher will set these expectations at nought and educate his public to the fiercer frenzies of the dramatic method—until his group is ready.

The following well-known chorus from *Atalanta in Calydon* has not been chosen, any more than the Auden chorus, for its suitability for any age group; indeed, like the Auden it is essentially adult or sixth-form work. I have chosen it because it demonstrates obviously and insistently those qualities that require the tonal approach:

> When the hounds of spring are on winter's traces,
> The mother of months in meadow or plain
> Fills the shadows and windy places
> With lisp of leaves and ripple of rain;
> And the brown bright nightingale amorous
> Is half assuaged for Itylus,
> For the Thracian ships and the foreign faces,
> The tongueless vigil, and all the pain.
>
> .    .    .    .    .
>
> And Pan by noon and Bacchus by night,
> Fleeter of foot than the fleet-foot kid,
> Follows with dancing and fills with delight
> The Maenad and the Bassarid;
> And soft as lips that laugh and hide
> The laughing leaves of the trees divide,
> And screen from seeing and leave in sight
> The god pursuing, the maiden hid.
>
> The ivy falls with the Bacchanal's hair
> Over her eyebrows hiding her eyes;
> The wild vine slipping down leaves bare
> Her bright breast shortening into sighs;
> The wild vine slips with the weight of its leaves,
> But the berried ivy catches and cleaves
> To the limbs that glitter, the feet that scare
> The wolf that follows, the fawn that flies.

The most obvious thing to say about this poem is that it was conceived as sound. There is no real dramatic shape; but there are quite certainly many lines that ask for the best that voice can give them. To say aloud 'The man who madly drinks' is a dramatic problem; a great deal of effort has to be put into one word, 'madly'. 'With lisp of leaves and ripple of rain' is a phonetic problem, and so is 'The Maenad and the Bassarid'.

These are the positive signs. What are the negative ones? Well, suppose one argues for a dramatic approach to one or two suitable lines. Suppose one tries to separate pursued and pursuer in

> And soft as lips that laugh and hide
> The laughing leaves of the trees divide,
> And screen from seeing and leave in sight
> The god pursuing, the maiden hid.

What happens then? For a start the whole stanza will no longer be intoxicating: it will become merely coy. Secondly, the unity of the scene will be disrupted, both in its unity of meaning and in its undoubted unity of sound. Thirdly, one cannot intrude real drama without making the whole thing ludicrous. In the Auden poem 'The handshake', 'the cough', 'the kiss' are words that represent actualities and to give them their full meaning at least a hint of the actuality, or of the dramatic atmosphere behind the actuality, must come into the speaking of the word. But a line as delicately poised as

> 'And soft as lips that laugh and hide'

cannot be interrupted by any suggestion of immediacy. One could break the verse up between two voices with some effect, perhaps; but to break it up between two groups of voices and at the same time deny any dramatic spontaneity and vigour to the dramatic performance of a dramatic conception would be fatal.

Having decided that the poem is suitable for the tonal method then, and for this only, how should one set about presenting it?

Earlier I used the phrase 'sculpt in sound', and it is apt. The statue does not exist before the stone; nor does the choral speech exist before the teacher has assembled the total note of all the voices at his disposal.

In the classroom the teacher is not a producer. That is important. He has not selected his voices, as he would for a chorus in a play, nor can he have any preconceived effect in mind until he knows his group.

This is very fortunate because it prevents his trying to be an expert. Expert producers bore the class: they keep thirty people sitting still while elaborate instructions are given to 'you, you, and you'; and because they *are* instructions there is no sense of growth.

Therefore, the sensible teacher will hear the whole group read the poem first. If it is a large class he will make them read very quietly and rhythmically so that he can control them; if it is a small group then everyone can be encouraged to read vigorously.

He will resist any idea of obtaining a high degree of co-ordination. Ideally his natural choice of anapaest or dactyl will impose its own conformity; in any event a group of voices very quickly grows to itself—witness the co-ordination obtained by a thousand children saying the Lord's Prayer. A teacher who tries to beat his group into time is inviting boredom. So is a teacher who says that certain words are indistinct and insists on the class saying them until he is satisfied. There will be no unifying rhythmic impulse, so he never will be satisfied.

Instead he accepts a rather uncouth block of sound and wonders how to shape it. If it is for public performance he can take his time; if it is merely a class activity then he must maintain the momentum of the lesson.

The best way to do this is to shed some voices quickly from different parts of the poem, perhaps leaving an obvious sound crescendo in one verse, building up to a crescendo in a line elsewhere, and also seeking a good diminuendo, or even just a very quiet or whispered line:

> With lisp of leaves and ripple of rain.

Then having made these brief and elementary dispositions he sets the class off again.

Ideally, once the teacher has begun the process of shaping, he should leave as much as possible to class suggestion. If the class members are used to the dramatic method they should be very eager to advise; if they are not, then they should not be essaying the tonal approach.

However, one often does meet with a greater dullness in the class with this method, and there are two easy devices with which it can be overcome. One is to abdicate at once from any position of artistic authority. One can say something like, 'That sounded rather rough from here. Will you come out and listen to it, Thompson and Wilmott?' Then make the group say it again and pass the problem to Thompson and Wilmott. They may find some intelligent answers or they may not. Generally the rest of the form will resent being bossed for long by two of its number and will start offering counter advice. Controlled democracy provides as good an impulse as any, and slowly the poem improves.

A far far better approach, which is equally entertaining when one is essaying the dramatic method, is to use a tape-recorder. Let the group hear a play-back of the very first reading; they are then in a position to judge it objectively. The recording always stimulates activity, and it also provides a record of the progress made and the paths taken.

I find this especially important when one is trying to link classroom with concert platform. A group can experiment wildly and excessively if each stage is recorded on the tape. There is no ridiculous point of arrival. If they overshoot perfection it does not matter: they can come back to it. They can hear all of their ideas in turn and then fasten on the best for performance. A tape-recorder is a stimulus for any sort of dramatic activity.

So much for the classroom. Are there any techniques to be tried by the purist which are not likely to be suggested by the class? If I wished to answer this dishonestly it would be perfectly easy to crib any set of ideas offered by a class in a given lesson and reproduce them as my own. However, I will deal justly.

An essential for polished rather than just adventurous work with the tonal method is to have one's class divided in one's mind into two main voice groups. If it is a co-educational class the problem is solved in advance; if it is not then one needs to make a division between lighter and heavier voices. It is tempting, if one does a lot of choral speech, to keep these groups constant, so that one can say merely that Group A will perform one activity and Group B another. This is very much a matter for the individual teacher and the individual group. If they can become Group A and Group B without becoming too clear about why they are so allocated then it is a satisfactory enough solution. Obviously in a girls' school one does not want to train a half-chorus of harmonious but hearty voiced teenagers to roar; any more than one wants to encourage boys to coo. An abnormal voice is an embarrassment; and a pupil is not happy to display abnormality for the sake of choral speech. It is best to dissemble. One can quickly read off one's list at the start of the lesson, keeping a few names as floaters to disguise basic distinctions; or, better, one can have permanent groups of unequal numbers. The hearty voiced can be far more numerous; the inferences will then be mathematical rather than physical. This may seem a lengthy digression; but in fact if one's whole teaching method depends upon persuading one's pupils to exhibit themselves then one needs to keep faith with them and try not to let them feel they are exhibiting themselves foolishly. As adults we have learnt to live with our voices. The boy whose voice is breaking (or stubbornly refusing to break) or the girl who sounds shrill or deep, is often far more sensitive than we can easily realize. We are not dealing with actors; therefore the voices are not instruments. We are attempting to educate by means of choral speech, not attain immediate perfection. The shy person, or the pupil worried about his voice, can develop his command of his tongue, and through that his self-confidence, easily enough in tonal choric speech if he is allowed to merge happily with the group.

Once one has developed a liking for the tonal method as a new activity, or if one is dealing with an adult group, a number of defined techniques are required. Vowelling is an important aspect of good choral speaking and one should be able to convey one's requirements simply if melopeia is to emerge in performance. Double 'O' (u:) is one's most dramatic vowel and poets generally hope for it to be hit hard:

—On Troy's *doom*-crimson shore,—

and some of our poetically overworked words like 'June', 'moon', 'lagoon', and 'noon' incorporate it. Not unnaturally, however, so do others: 'spoon', 'goon'; and it is a strange fact that very few speakers manage to get the most from this sound without quavering on the brink of absurdity. If you tell your group that heavy vowelling is required make sure that they do not overdo it.

'S' is a consonant for the reader to be early aware of:

—With lisp of leaves and ripple of rain—

and the best practical approach with a group is to ask them to *say* the words with it in if you feel they are unnecessarily slowing, or ugly, and *hiss* the words in which you feel it is deliberate. Straightaway one has achieved a very telling effect with the difficult line I have just quoted. The two opposed onomatopeia are contrasted in speech without further effort.

Crescendo and diminuendo can employ techniques other than mere voice sensitivity. For example, a voice shut-off system is worth practising, so that over the last six words of a falling passage one can drop word by word from six voices to one.

Quick contrasts are always to be sought out.

> (Group) There is always a wicked secret.
> (One voice speaking monotonously) A private reason for
>     this.

This may seem unnecessarily technical; it may seem lightweight. Those who feel the former have my sympathy. They have only to go into the classroom and all will come plain. Those who feel the latter have my complete agreement. A competent class can concoct more dramatic and tonal ideas round a given poem in fifteen minutes than one can think up in cold blood in a fortnight. If a poem seems dull, try another quickly. At least, don't abandon the idea till you have attempted Auden's *Night Mail* by either method, or a blend of both. It is a poem that succeeds as choral speech with pupils of many ages.

If one is dealing with juniors it is perhaps hard to say where group participation ends and choral speaking begins; and certainly much of one's work will be confined to the dramatic approach. The tonal method is at a disadvantage here because it calls for rehearsal and rehearsal is the one thing juniors do not like. Coupled with action and mime, or treated as a sort of chanting game, it can be successful; but one's choice should be limited to work that requires rowdy rather than mellow effects:

> Trample! trample! went the roan,
> Trap! Trap! went the grey;
> But pad! pad! pad! like a thing that was mad,
> My chestnut broke away.

With the very young one merely elaborates on the well-known. Almost any nursery rhyme can have its action enriched by sound:

> *A boy:* Jack
> *A girl:*          and Jill
> *Together:*        went up the hill
> *Class:*  To fetch a pail of water.
> *Boy:*    Jack
> *Class (roar):*     fell down
> *Boy:*    and broke his crown
> *Girl:*   and Jill
> *Girls:*          came tumb-ell-ing after.

With classes of this age the teacher will always break up the suitable polysyllabic words, like 'tumbling' so that they become exciting phonetic units. It is a further step in an education in sound. One is really using both methods at once.

With older juniors tongue-twisters are a useful and amusing subject for the tonal approach, and one can even take a line and have it reiterated, diminuendo or crescendo, by different combinations of voices. In the chapter on Method the lesson I commended for this age was in fact based upon modified choral speech; and most poems suitable to the age group can be attempted chorally.

Young teenagers are difficult to introduce to the tonal approach: it is too conscious and deliberate an activity and gives them time for reflection. If one has a group which will perform *publicly* quite happily then the tonal approach can be tried. Performance is its own justification to many pupils for pre-performance agonies.

In this case, choose something massive that will call for plenty of group invention and that will also make some use of single voices. 'The Runnable Stag' is a splendid challenge, and it also enables the class to enjoy an aurally intoxicating poem that one dare not normally venture in the classroom. Unlike the Auden and the Swinburne, the two mature examples given, it has a narrative shape and a recognizable direction. Its bad point is its title.

> When the pods went pop on the broom, green broom,
>   And apples began to be golden-skinned,
> We harboured a stag in the Priory coomb,
>   And we feathered his trail up-wind, up-wind,
>   We feathered his trail up-wind—
>       A stag of warrant, a stag, a stag,
>       A runnable stag, a kingly crop,
>       Brow, bay and tray and three on top,
>       A stag, a runnable stag.
>
> Then the huntsman's horn rang yap, yap, yap,
>   And 'Forwards' we heard the harbourer shout;
> But 'twas only a brochet that broke a gap
>   In the beechen underwood, driven out,
>   From the underwood antlered out
>       By warrant and might of the stag, the stag,
>       The runnable stag, whose lordly mind
>       Was bent on sleep, though beamed and tined
>       He stood, a runnable stag.

The possibilities are already numerous and obvious, and it subsequently offers many changes of rhythm and mood as it

moves with breathless but deliberate beat to the point where
the stag

> —sank in the depths of the sea—
> The stag, the buoyant stag, the stag
> That slept at last in a jewelled bed
> Under the sheltering ocean spread,
> The stag, the runnable stag.

The metre is organic enough to hold voice against voice, but
the individual speech and sense units are brief, contrasting,
and clear. This is good tonal poetry, and the subject is sym-
pathetic.

If one hopes to employ a combination of dramatic and
tonal method—a very good technique with young teenagers
—then any narrative poem with a long refrain should offer
something. Ballad—and Song—books reward the searcher:

> With sour-featured Whigs the Grassmarket was crammed
> As if half the West had set tryst to be hanged;
> There was spite in each look, there was fear in each 'ee,
> As they watched for the Bonnets of Bonny Dundee,
>
> Come fill up my cup, come fill up my can,
> Come saddle your horses, and call up your men;
> Come ope the West Post, and let me gang free,
> And it's room for the bonnets of Bonny Dundee!

The themes are exciting, the rhythms canter delightfully and
in addition to the possibilities of the refrain, the tonal creeps
up in lines like:

> There's brass on the target of barken'd bull-hide;
> There's steel in the scabbard that dangles beside;
> The brass shall be burnished, the steel shall flash free,

This, rather than Tennyson's 'The mellow ouzel fluted in the elm', is teenage melopeia. Indeed, with this age one must beware of such lines, for they make words posture meaninglessly. Language should be thrust home more vigourously:

Not in silk nor in samet we lie, not in curtained solemnity die
Among women who chatter and cry, and children who
    mumble a prayer.
But we sleep by the ropes of the camp, and we rise with a
    shout, and we tramp
With the sun or the moon for a lamp, and the spray of the
    wind in our hair.

From the lands, where the elephants are, to the forts of Merou
    and Balghar,
Our steel we have brought and our star to shine on the ruins
    of Rum.
We have marched from the Indus to Spain, and by God we
    will go there again;
We have stood on the shore of the plain where the watchers
    of Destiny boom.
A mort of destruction we made at Jalula where men were
    afraid,
For death was a difficult trade, and the sword was a broker of
    doom.

In other words, one must remember the aversions of this age-group and introduce only language that is vigorous and functional, not merely ornamental.

At all times one must avoid what is stupid in the classroom. Nashe's famous

> 'Cuckoo, jug-jug, pu-we, to-witta-woo!'

and Lyly's often borrowed

> 'Jug, jug, jug, jug, tereu! she cries'

are not for any exponent of choral speech who values skin and reputation; nor is any other assemblage of animal noises. A group will 'thud' and 'clang' with reasonable abandon; a single 'Tu-wit, tu-woo' makes it all too aware of itself. Self-consciousness is a great enemy of choral speech.

This is because poetry is not merely *recited* by a group or an individual; it is *performed*. Recitation is a bore, performance an enjoyable activity. Therefore one should encourage certain of the trappings of performance. The monologue is easy enough. For after-school poetry meetings I allow people to dress the part. Quite recently I witnessed a very successful performance of John Betjeman's *Hunter Trials* by a boy decked in jodhpurs, riding-whip, pony hat and several large hanks of artificial hair, given to an appreciative audience of *three hundred schoolboys*. Of course, in a case like this the *poem must be humorous* and the audience *used to this sort of entertainment*; but both of these circumstances are well within normal control.

Choral speech, and individual performances, can also be accompanied by sound effects on occasions (though one's wildest ventures should be kept for the literary or dramatic club, rather than the classroom): a tinny piano often provides a good background for a bar-fight ballad, for example; pistol shots and hooves should also sound in all such humorous or mock horrific occasions; and the crescendo on the piano, beloved of the patrons of the silent cinema, should be encouraged to follow any pseudo-spine chilling or stalking verses.

One should also realize that the ballad is essentially a musical creation, and encourage sung performances. One will be lucky to gain much from border ballads in this way, but a single mention of skiffle or the Deep South brings fans by the hundred.

For seniors many of these more elaborate or plainly vigorous sessions are an after-school problem, but when one has encouraged the idea that poetry is a club activity, and that a poetry club is a diverse and interesting experience much has been achieved. A comic verse play, a sung ballad, a group composition (rhyming and generally humorous, and here given its rehearsed performance in full dress) another ballad to the guitar, a rehearsed monologue, some skiffle, a comic piece of rehearsed choral speech, more skiffle, a few short light poems, and any sort of popular finale—such an evening will be widely supported several times a term. I mention it in the context of choral speech, because I think one's pupils catch the whole idea of uninhibited performance from here more than anywhere else.

Juniors are far more used to make-believe, and one can achieve much more of this sort in one's normal teaching periods, except that the teenage pastimes will obviously have to be abandoned. Remember that, at the Junior School Concert, poetic villains need a burnt-cork moustache quite as much as prosaic ones, and if choral speech is to be attempted, see that it is something where the group can dress as cowboys, or red indians, or engine-drivers—or *something*. And give them some sound effects.

Lastly: good work in any of these directions is always worth committing to the tape-recorder. We must cherish what fires we have. A brilliantly funny or gusty piece of work by their fellows, even thirty seconds of recorded brilliance, will do more to stimulate a fresh class than any amount of talking. The best thing about the methods mentioned in this book is that the teacher talks very little. After all, the teacher is the only weak point in the argument. And since it implies the fullest class participation, the importance of choral speech to all of one's creative activities will be obvious: it enables poetry, whether written by the pupils themselves or by established poets, to be richly experienced. Creation and performance are key factors in English teaching, and choral speech offers these in no uncertain measure.

But its true value is in its sense of celebration, not of poetry but of poetic activity. Poetry in itself is not important; but the enjoyment of poetry is. Class participation in poetry, once it is created, is nowhere so vital as when it is being exploited aloud as vigorous sound. If the class is able to experience poetry fully its taste will mature rapidly; it will modify both its creative and its critical standards; it will exploit and exhaust what it has and set up a demand for more. One hopes that the class will come to set poems aside not because they have been imperfectly perceived but because they have been perceived to be imperfect. Choral speech enables pupils to do this both with their own work and with the work of others. It represents restless activity, born of self-expression and communal impulse.

Activity may be an illusion; but it is from this illusion that one derives the energy necessary for progress.

# 9. EXAMINING

THIS SUBJECT requires a separate chapter almost as much as a smallpox case needs quarantine. One has to prevent the feeling of anger and frustration that the whole question arouses from contaminating one's other judgments. If one's teaching in the smallest degree takes notice of terminal examinations, Ordinary Level, or Advanced Level, until such notice is inevitable, then everything said so far in this book will become meaningless. Terminal examinations, however, can and should be made to play their part in the plan: it is the General Certificate of Education, and indeed Public Examinations in general, that are the real menace. Let us consider these first.

Books on brain-washing are instructive here. So far every book I have read by people who have survived this disgusting process has offered the same formula for survival. The victim must seek to retain a feeling of moral superiority towards his tormentors; he must see them as representing not only an inferior but a separate order of being; he must not only recoil from their vileness but be careful that he does not fall merely into a rhythm of revulsion dictated by them. At no point must their patterns coincide, not even as boundaries of separation.

So it is with pupil and examiner. If poetry is to survive the public examination the teacher must continue to urge that the examination is concerned neither with the enjoyment of poetry nor with poetry itself. The examiner will not ask questions that are concerned with either.

## In Particular

Consider these questions:

What impressions have you formed from *Poetry and Prose* of Tennyson as a man?

What does this mean and what does it achieve other than the intrusion of that anaemic figure, the poet, into his poems, where he does not belong?
Still better:

Contrast life at the court of King Francis as depicted in *The Glove* with that at the court of King Arthur as revealed in *Morte D'Arthur*.

This is Ordinary Level, so the pupil is asked merely to regard the poem as a catalogue of facts. Now even if the facts required related in any material way to the substance of the poem this would be a pernicious question; but, in reality, they do not. Perhaps the examiner would like to explain what references there are in *Morte D'Arthur* that would give even an intelligent mature pupil, like himself, any material for such an answer. Even when I read the poem his way with his question in mind I still only found two or three half-lines that suggested anything at all.

It is not the examiner's fault that *The Glove* is a bad poem, though somebody must have decided that it should be inflicted on several thousands of candidates; but, really, the court of King Francis is not described in the poem at all; nothing is described. The poet, in the person of Ronsard, is at pains to tell you he is not going to describe things because he is not Clement Marot. His concern is with the actions of men. Certain things about the Court may be inferred from actions just as we may infer 'fish shop' from 'selling fish', but if statements are made about selling fish it is ridiculous to test our understanding of them by asking us about the shop in which the fish is sold.

Now none of this is the examiner's fault. He is, after all, an examiner, with an inherited tradition behind him. He has to think up new questions; and to defend any wrong choices he can claim that the examinee has the same tradition behind him, the tradition of twisting the text to suit his own particular sermon. If the pupil does this cunningly enough the examiner will give him credit for it. If he goes on doing it cunningly he may be an examiner himself one day. Poetry will have suffered, but what of that?

After all, at higher levels we accept such questions as 'How many children had Lady Macbeth?'. We begin by saying something like 'Shakespeare does not answer the question he so skilfully poses; but if we consider how the question is put and why the answer is withheld we shall come very near to understanding the final intentions of the play'. We do not believe our last assertion, and the examiner does not believe in anything to do with the whole question. He is like the king of Lilliput watching the gymnastics of his courtiers so that he can decide on the suitability for promotion in quite another field.

This is not a digression. I said in my very first chapter that our bad habits as teachers are ingrained and engrafted from the day when we were pupils. Many of us are still pupils in higher systems that are no less pernicious than the ones that have already made us what we are.

Let us go back to our own pupils, who are the only people who can teach us educational rights, because educational wrongs have not yet ruined them. From their point of view there are four things wrong with public examinations in poetry:

> the candidates have to study closely
> for an extended period of time
> poetry they did not choose to read
> and that has probably been badly chosen.

Add to this the fact that they know that this effort leads to an examination vital to their future, an examination, moreover, in which they will be asked merely stupid questions. Add also the fact that we as teachers have a prime duty, moral if not educational, to see that they know the poems well enough, and in the way the examiner wants, so that they may answer the examiner's questions, and the problem assumes rather alarming proportions.

What can we do about this?

In the long run we can hope either that poetry will not be set in such examinations, a defeatist and very likely vain wish, or that a better sort of poetry will be included—that is, a less pretentious poetry suited to the age group in the case of Ordinary Level, and that more reasonable questions will be asked. One understands, however, that most examining bodies nowadays include poetry merely in order to keep it before the pupil's eye, whatever this means.

There is another reasonable suggestion, already adopted by many schools, and that is that their pupils do not take the literature examination now it is no longer compulsory. Not much would seem to be lost by this since drama and prose are as badly treated as poetry; but most schools use this as an excuse for not reading literature in the relevant years. Educationally this is indefensible; and it can be objected to on practical grounds: the pupil needs a satisfactory literary background if he is to succeed in his language paper. Besides, as a pupil progresses, at least as an Arts student, he has at some point or other to get on the literary band-wagon. However, if one omits the literature paper it still remains likely that the masses will not lose, and may even retain some of their diminishing enthusiasms.

Suppose one is committed to such papers as they are.

The first thing the schoolmaster ought to do is consider all of the alternatives, for it will be found that most examining bodies do offer alternative evils. London University at Ordinary Level, for example, offers an indefensible Methuen selection of modern poetry, none of the poets in which have been dead for more than fifty years, and none of whom were ever exactly 'mainstream', to borrow a term from jazz, but in which a very few poems might be found by a good man to justify the book to a good class. If such a man were really convinced he could even teach it by the anthology gambit mentioned in another chapter, that is by refusing to teach it.

They offer *Absolom and Achitophel,* a work which most people over twenty-five find magnificent and which is therefore quite unlikely to appeal to the antipathetic age-group it is intended for. However, this is so far removed from what well-taught pupils have come to regard as poetry by this age that it is possible that another good man, with somewhat cynical aspirations, might teach it as a something else.

They offer some Keats' selections, not a brilliant choice, but it is a fact that girls at least become Keatsian a little sooner than boys and suffer even longer. So possibly girls can have a rather vicarious enjoyment of Keats instilled; experts always suggest its feasibleness, but it has never even looked possible in the case of any girls classes I have seen. They prefer masculine art, provided it is not exaggeratedly masculine. None of this is meant to attack Keats, merely Keats at sixteen.

And lastly they offer four longer poems: *The Rime of the Ancient Mariner, Morte D'Arthur, Sohrab and Rustum,* and *The Glove.* This is a very reasonable sort of choice, even though three of the four works are now only literary curiosities, so the selection is going to be changed next year. That is, it is as reasonable as such a choice can ever be, since it is not the class's choice, and the poems need to be studied in detail for the examination.

Ideally, one needs to allow or to seem to allow one's pupils to study which of the alternatives appeals to them. At Advanced Level, with small classes, it is frequently possible to let the matter rest as an individual choice: the pupils can each do as they wish and be divided up into suitable tutorial groups. But for Ordinary Level, with its large classes, one cannot do this. Whether one can for adult Ordinary Level students at evening classes depends rather more upon local circumstances.

It may be, from flexible, fortuitous or indulgent buying of stock, that one can offer the class a genuine choice, spending a week with all the evidence before them to accept or reject. This is the ideal. More than likely one will only be able to produce one or two alternatives and be compelled to explain away the rest. Or one may have to rely upon talk entirely.

In every case be completely honest, not only about the poetry, but about the exam. This attitude has been implicit in every technique I have so far discussed and the class should come to expect it as a matter of course. Paint the books, fairly and squarely, and advance a personal opinion. Then talk about the needs of the exam. Try to separate as quickly as possible the ideas of 'good poem' and 'good poem for the exam'. Establish a barrier between sensitivity and exam technique.

Once the class chooses, it will be at least *with* the poem to some extent. If you think the poem is bad, and something quite different from what the class has previously come to enjoy, *say so*. Keep 'poetry' intact at all costs.

As one progresses with factual techniques and correspondingly emphasizes their unreality, the class will become critically more aware. It is the first occasion on which it has been confronted with conflicting values and this is an important moment. Out of this dualistic approach comes the moral superiority I spoke about earlier.

It is quite likely, however, that one will have to sit back and watch a great poem become a sour topic with the class. It is here that one's own position, as well as theirs, becomes ambiguous. The class attack—and there must be free discussion by this age—will fall not only upon bad poetry, not only upon a bad system, but upon a good and great poem, and by implication upon all your own teaching has stood for.

Part of the answer is that one's own teaching should have *seemed* to stand for no such thing, however much it moved towards such a result. All one can do otherwise is attempt to benefit from the new atmosphere of non-aggressive honesty and say that in fact it does seem to be a fine and important poem, that obviously it won't appeal to everybody, but its main appeal is . . .

It is here for the first time that some sense of the history of taste can be encouraged. Everything advocated earlier about the unrelated teaching of poetry will have kept such considerations firmly in the background. The point was made, however, that the present is the best springboard to the past; with sixteen-year-old pupils the leap should be encouraged.

Progress is always the aim, for progress means momentum. To put the matter as negatively as possible, a class kept away from academic and formal instruction until the ages of fifteen may well find the change to it a satisfying and temporally invigorating experience. However, I believe that the principles advocated throughout this book will still be found correct and that there is no need for such shock tactics.

For years the class has been encouraged to see poetry as modern, vigorous, spontaneous, even rebellious. Their own poetry represents doing as they please. It is not hard to depict the poets of earlier generations as 'doing as they please'. No matter how stultiloquential the idiom that the examining board visits upon them it is generally easy enough to find something even 'less modern' and demonstrate a sequent superiority.

What does the exam teach? It teaches growth, contrast, and a fresh objectiveness. It can be a challenge.

All teaching for examinations involves a certain sleight and deception. With a good class, a grammar school top-stream, I always read far more poetry than the examination prescribes. I also try to satisfy such classes' dynamic zest for mere information. Fact in literature may be mere fancy, but try to withhold fact from a pupil brimful of chemistry formulae, dates, sketch-maps, and other—to the pupil—highly competitive information, and he will regard one's evasiveness as mere incompetence. And, in a wider sense, so it is.

After all, the whole problem involved in teaching poetry for an exam is that there is very little to say about a poem, if you are honest. A charlatan, of the sort English teaching produces in great numbers, can disseminate a great deal of bogus material, however; and it is tempting to be a charlatan.

Sooner or later the class needs to learn the labels I warned against in the chapter on aims: the tags of scansion, figures of speech, stanza-forms, and other such mesmeric mumbo-jumbo which will quickly lead it from the poem itself.

But even here, with the examination looming, the basic empiric principle must not be ignored. We must not say: 'And here, at line five, is a metaphor.' For a start the pupils must become familiar with the poem as a whole: its general progresses and larger structures must be appreciated first. Then they must discover the individual 'devices' (and even that word can reveal a dangerous habit of mind) for themselves. When they see the nature of the device they can ask for its label, if they do not already know it.

The chances are, however, that they *will* know it. If composition has been developed properly they will have assimilated 'the whole bag of tricks' because the formal properties of verse will have come in a comic context in their previous year; and now, as they re-apply themselves to poetry, as an identity far more fundamental. After all, they will be coming to the examination poetry as craftsmen.

## *Examining*

This is by nature sketchy, because it would be impossible
to fill in for other people and other classes the means by which
this widening appreciation is achieved. The final injection of
knowledge is a technical problem.

There is one genuine insoluble, however: the examination
answer. I have attempted a number of different approaches to
this with different classes, and as I write now I am waiting for
the post to bring me the statistic half-answer to my latest
attempt. In the end, I know, the answer must be the one given
in the chapter on Making. In fairness to the pupils one must
teach it as a technique. One defends this as the only answer to
the impossible situation. If the pupils have not been surfeited
with essays already, they will recognize it as quite a useful
intellectual exercise. If they have been reared on the essay they
will not need to be taught to write examination answers,
though they may need to be taught English.

School examinations in poetry occupy an ambiguous posi-
tion. One cannot examine the Arts, and therefore the more
successfully one teaches them the less of them there is for
examination; the more nearly one approaches a correct sense
of enjoyment through creation of the Art of Poetry, the more
will the Science of Poetry—its examinable identity—tend to
be dissipated. Or that is the theory.

In fact one should weigh certain other considerations
against this, and remember that if an ideal cannot be attained
then that which is closest to the ideal is not always the best
substitute. Regard the present educational system how we
will, we cannot omit any one part of it without risking that
part.

Examinations are an important aspect of all our higher
systems, and in spite of certain arguable imperfections it is
unlikely that we shall see anything better in their place. And
once a subject exists in an examination context, it is dangerous

in the extreme to make it a non-examination subject. If the
system at large extols certain values one cannot openly argue
to a class that some activities cannot be gauged according to
those values. To be non-materialistic in a materialist world is
to be considered immaterial.

This seems very negative, but is it? I believe that from the
point of view of the class it is not negative in the least. If one
can abolish examinations in the Arts, as one can in some
modern schools, then by all means abolish them; if not one
has to make the very best that one can of them. The best can
be very good indeed, so good that they can often be a most
important part of one's teaching.

A schoolmaster whom I very much admire was once sitting
with some examination scripts, looking very depressed. I do
not know whether his comment was original: it was certainly
honest. He said: 'This has been a very bad examination paper.
Nobody has learnt anything by answering the questions.'

*Nobody has learnt anything by answering the questions.* A good
examination paper, whatever its subject, always demands a
certain amount of creative thought from the examinee. That
is, it should always seek to utilize the expected tension to make
the pupil force his mind through an unexpected problem.

If this is true of all subjects, how much more true must it
be of the Arts, where, in a sense, all that one can present the
pupil is the freshness of the problem. At the very least in an
examination, one should set a *stimulating* and *challenging* paper
and praise the results, however disappointing, rather than a
simple paper that leads one to derision at the expense of
obvious error.

The English teacher should be able to progress well beyond
this simple educational truth, which is after all open to every-
one. He should be able to produce a paper that his pupils will
enjoy tackling. He knows his pupils' tastes by now.

His compositions can be on their most fruitful subjects.

Dan Dare can be sent to Saturn, or the class can be invited to finish anecdotes that begin 'Scarcely had the shots rung out when the high-powered sedan went purring away from the Bank'. The passage for comprehension can be lurid or amusing, so can any poem set for comment. Any correction of sentences can be of humorous utterances, and some of the mistakes should be enormous enough to provoke relaxed amusement.

There is nothing original here. Every English teacher in the country does much the same thing with his general questions, and this sort of examination, I contend, does little harm to one's poetry.

The ideal is not to abolish the examination, but to extend these basic processes as vigorously as possible.

The class ought always to choose what poems they wish to be examined on. One nomination each provides a fair list, but one that individuals still feel they have chosen. With junior forms I also add about six poems written by members of the class and sometimes one group poem.

There are always people unhappy about this, but it is a perfectly rational position. Examination is either to test knowledge or appreciation. It is not worth *knowing* the literature that is generally thought suitable for junior classes, and appreciation is the best guarantee of later learning. Appreciation is best developed on the basis of what the class likes, and it likes what it writes.

The following questions give an idea of what can be asked:

List some of the poems you have enjoyed reading this term, and briefly defend your liking for three or four of them.

Are there any poems you have not enjoyed reading? What was wrong with them?

## In Particular

> Here is a poem written by John Brown who was in this
> class last year. What do you think of it? Compare it with
> any poem you have written recently.

In the first two questions the pupil is encouraged to write
about several poems. A good pupil will remember details; a
bad pupil will at least remember something. Memory is not
being tested. To concentrate on single poems implies that
memory of detail is all important. It is hardly necessary to
point out that by being educated in the 'feel' of poetry pupils
will in time come to develop a retentive mind without being
made to 'learn for the exam'.

The vocabulary of questions is important. 'Defend' is a
personal word: 'give your reasons', or worse 'state your
reasons' are impersonal phrases. They imply that evidence is
about to be assessed. 'Defend' may seem a back-against-the-
wall-word, but in fact it is one to which we all respond.
Besides it puts the pupil 'on the spot' very reasonably. It is
surprising how many previously lukewarm pupils start
'defending' poems after the exams that they would not have
considered at all readable before. As I suggested earlier, a large
part of one's technique is the manœuvring of pupils until they
catch at a standard. They rarely let go again; their egos are
involved. Similarly, in the last question, I ask: 'What do you
think of it?'

In the case of the antipathetic question I go further. 'What
was wrong with them?' The pupil must be confident and feel
that he has the right to be confident. His reasons are absolute.
I have seen in such cases 'Give your reasons, if any', and 'Try
to support your argument by means of close reference to the
text'.

'Close reference to the text' is the usual examination tag.
It is meant to avoid what examiners call 'wool'. The fact that
'wool' is what most people see when they read a poem makes

examiners see red. Examiners prefer Miltonic Inversions to the Absolute At Large.

There are certain questions that should never be set. I think it is wrong to ask a pupil to scan a stanza: it is hard to see what scansion does for anyone, except destroy his perception of every other quality in a poem. 'Well-taught' pupils nearly always complain, 'It doesn't scan,' when faced with a new poem. By the time they arrive at university it generally becomes their only formula for answering anything. Personally I have never found any good poem that really 'scans' according to the recognized methods; though all good poems are undeniably metrically or rhythmically 'right'.

The division into 'feet' is especially meaningless. A line works by overall weight. It is a good man indeed—I've met him and very proud he is of his ability—who can tell the difference between an anapaestic line with a feminine ending and a normal dactylic line. And I've heard very learned arguments, conducted on the one hand by the occupier of a professorial chair, as to whether 'One Word More' is written in trochees or whether it's 'just' blank verse with a repeated feminine ending. An interesting case of vacant possession. Even if one deals merely with 'stress' it can only give the pupil about a quarter of the *metrical* pattern, for quantity is so important as well. And the metrical pattern is only a very small part of the overall sound pattern, and the overall sound pattern. . . . A poem is what it is and what it means.

What it means to the pupil.

The pupil must not be asked: to paraphrase a poem; to find metaphors; to express images in his own words; to perform any purely mechanical tasks with the poem at all.

It is not a jigsaw puzzle. Though from the way poetry is taught one would often think so. People who think that this sort of question should be asked—50 per cent of the people who teach English—would be well advised to take a very long walk and ask themselves why. It teaches the pupil nothing: it teaches the teacher very little about the pupil except that he has certain scavenging aptitudes. He is fast being educated to the point where he will become a perfectly contented picker of gooseberries on a soft-fruit farm. Gooseberries are a well-concealed fruit and uniform with the bush. I'm all for teaching gooseberry-pickers poetry, but not for having poetry teach them gooseberry-picking.

The real test of a teacher as the examiner of his pupil' works is how he marks their answers. Even one's choice of implement is important, strange as it may seem to the person who scrawls 'nonsense' in 5B pencil across every other answer, and sets his graphite hoof-print on the corner of every page. The Science Master who blazoned in blunt red crayon 'VERY GOOD 10/10 ! ! !' right across my notes, obliterating my own priggish and anaemic records so proudly kept, confirmed me as an Arts student in my most wavering hours. An equally ham-fisted English master—had there been one—would have brushed me back to Science.

The marking of anything that has taken a pupil's time should be done as politely as possible. A pupil cannot be made more neat than he is, but he *can* be kept to his own standard; and so should a teacher keep to his own standard. If a pupil is not giving his best then there is something wrong with the teaching *or with the general attitude of the pupil*. Neither of these things can be successfully dealt with by adverse, disgruntled, or irreverent marking.

I believe, after some thought and experiment, that neat, helpful and encouraging comments in red ink are the best, even if this is the traditional answer. They are far less disfiguring than red ball-point, red crayon (an abomination), all other inks and all other pencils. There are excellent arguments for the use of hard pencil; it represents unobtrusive, even camouflaged comments. It also looks horribly scruffy.

Errors are best indicated with a single red dot rather than a line. Elaborate marginal codes waste everyone's time; but 'Sp' for spelling and 'Gr' for grammar are useful enough. Marking can be more personal than this if it is humorously rather than sarcastically so. I always enjoyed the comments of the master who wrote 'Come off it', 'Nark it', and 'Oi', though I now feel it is most unwise to be slangily familiar. I did not respond too happily to 'Disgusting!', 'O Puerility!', and 'Oaf!' Nor does anyone else.

However much one falsifies marks as propaganda for encouragement during term, in the exam they must be absolute. It should be realized that pupils regard mark-lists as sacred, however cynically they have been arrived at.

Nevertheless marks are a rather disquieting experience for everyone concerned. Their principal disadvantage is that they encourage the good and discourage the bad, and there is nothing much one can do about it. For an Arts subject I think very little is lost by having a very small range in any numerical mark scheme, and I always concentrate closely on the median. This means that I can always demonstrate to the worst pupil, however falsely, that a little more effort would have bettered him considerably. Marks cannot be scrambled but they can be squeezed, so that the worst do not feel the best beyond them.

Letter, token, and other schemes of assessment—rather than formal-marking—are obviously better educationally, and would be especially good for a delicately poised subject like poetry; but they are not sound administratively, and what the pupil gains in propaganda he loses in terms of justice.

However one marks, it should be a positive rather than a negative action. 'This is worth 12': not, 'This has eight mistakes'. To deduct for error as an exclusive system leads to gross injustices, besides representing a dangerous frame of mind. It is possible for the 'Cat-sat-on-the-mat' sort of work to earn full marks and for genuine endeavour to earn nothing. Many teachers of English complain that it is difficult to recognize genuine endeavour. We are so mark-obsessed that this complaint is common. My advice to anyone who is unwilling to give his pupils the benefit of the doubt is to shoot himself.

Marks always cause much trouble, even when they have been satisfactorily arrived at. Different subjects involve different marking problems, and the teacher who has worked out his private educational formula is frequently told to 'scale them up, scale them down, spread them, compress them' before they are acceptable for the school mark sheet. This should be resisted.

Too many important educational decisions are taken as the result of figures on a piece of paper. Too many headmasters and head mistresses want to say 'all pupils with totals from 740 to 820 will go in stream X' without further debate. A pupil may be 90/16th in one subject and 50/top in another. Both of those marks have been arrived at by intelligent people who know the needs of their subject, and see how an examination can best serve their subject and their class. It is not the task of statistics to resolve what is a personal and not a statistical problem. One generally knows that a reasonable attempt has been made, in so far as promotion is ever entirely reasonable, if a pupil with 750 is out, and another one with 720 in.

This is not poetry, surely? If you can go into a school and separate your subject from all this you are a very lucky person. Poetry is only possible when the subject is at ease.

The relationships within the subject should be fair: I have always insisted so. Poetry is hard to separate from non-poetry if the teaching is good and the attitude correct, and it will not be treated differently from the rest of the subject. Similar questions must be asked on every branch of literature and composition, and ideally literature and composition should be made to blur. Past composition is literature and can be remembered for an exam. Literature can be made to challenge composition. 'Here is a poem by Gray. Do you think you're better? Why?' A poem can be compared with a piece of prose. The injecting of pupils' own work saves poetry losing from the artificial comparisons mentioned in the chapter on Method.

Many people will disagree with this. Of course it is not the only answer. But all of the correct answers will be found to have certain similarities. They will be examinations set by people with a clear aim, together with a desire to educate by examining (this is only the formal counterpart of the class-room 'teaching by asking') and an unwillingness to test un-related mechanical skills. Their examination will not be con-cerned primarily with memory, and because of this their teaching will not have anticipated the examination. There will have been no formal revision; how can one 'revise' literature?

The pupils will find, and expect to find, their paper chal-lenging and entertaining, and they will know as they write that their work will be marked with courtesy and with some respect for the dignity of error. They know, as in any ordinary lesson, that they are creating something that will not be for-gotten, that will be discussed afterwards and that . . .

Oh no, I forgot. Most education authorities insist that their answer papers should be filed away and kept for assessment by the inspectors.

The pupil must be made to enjoy creating this statistic.

# INDEX

For Product Safety Concerns and Information please contact our EU
representative  GPSR@taylorandfrancis.com
Taylor & Francis Verlag GmbH, Kaufingerstraße 24, 80331 München, Germany